MW00559977

LIGHTNING PATHS

NCTE Editorial Board

Steven Bickmore

Catherine Compton-Lilly

Deborah Dean

Antero Garcia

Bruce McComiskey

Jennifer Ochoa

Staci M. Perryman-Clark

Anne Elrod Whitney

Vivian Yenika-Agbaw

Kurt Austin, Chair, ex officio

Emily Kirkpatrick, ex officio

Lightning Paths

75 Poetry Writing Exercises

Kyle Vaughn
Pulaski Academy, Little Rock, Arkansas

National Council of Teachers of English
1111 W. Kenyon Road, Urbana, Illinois 61801-1096
www.ncte.org

Staff Editor: Bonny Graham
Manuscript Editor: The Charlesworth Group
Interior Design: Jenny Jensen Greenleaf
Cover Design and Calligraphy: Barbara Yale-Read

NCTE Stock Number: 28213; eStock Number: 28237
ISBN 978-0-8141-2821-3; eISBN 978-0-8141-2823-7

©2018 by the National Council of Teachers of English.

All rights reserved. No part of this publication may be reproduced or transmitted in any form or by any means, electronic or mechanical, including photocopy, or any information storage and retrieval system, without permission from the copyright holder. Printed in the United States of America.

It is the policy of NCTE in its journals and other publications to provide a forum for the open discussion of ideas concerning the content and the teaching of English and the language arts. Publicity accorded to any particular point of view does not imply endorsement by the Executive Committee, the Board of Directors, or the membership at large, except in announcements of policy, where such endorsement is clearly specified.

NCTE provides equal employment opportunity (EEO) to all staff members and applicants for employment without regard to race, color, religion, sex, national origin, age, physical, mental or perceived handicap/disability, sexual orientation including gender identity or expression, ancestry, genetic information, marital status, military status, unfavorable discharge from military service, pregnancy, citizenship status, personal appearance, matriculation or political affiliation, or any other protected status under applicable federal, state, and local laws.

Every effort has been made to provide current URLs and email addresses, but because of the rapidly changing nature of the Web, some sites and addresses may no longer be accessible.

Library of Congress Cataloging-in-Publication Data

Names: Vaughn, Kyle, author.
Title: Lightning paths : 75 poetry writing exercises / Kyle Vaughn, Pulaski Academy, Little Rock, Arkansas.
Description: Urbana, Illinois : National Council of Teachers of English, [2018] | Includes bibliographical references.
Identifiers: LCCN 2018028664 (print) | LCCN 2018043722 (ebook) | ISBN 9780814128237 (ebook) | ISBN 9780814128213 | ISBN 9780814128237 (eISBN)
Subjects: LCSH: Poetry—Authorship—Problems, exercises, etc. | Poetry—Study and teaching. | English language—Composition and exercises.
Classification: LCC PN1059.A9 (ebook) | LCC PN1059.A9 V38 2018 (print) | DDC 808.1—dc23
LC record available at https://lccn.loc.gov/2018028664

Contents

Acknowledgments

I would like to thank . . .

My wife, Natalie, and my children, Eli, Charlotte, and Runa, for their love and for encouraging me and allowing me the time to finish this book.

My mother, my father, and my brother, Curt.

These former colleagues at the Hockaday School and Parish Episcopal School, who shaped my teaching and my life: Ayaz Pirani, Jason Mazzella, Michael Flickinger, Barbara Orlovsky, Janet Bilhartz, Kathryn Hodgkinson, Jim Wasserman, Andre Stipanovic, Colleen Durkin, Juliette McCullough, Sharon Childs, Marc Addington, Tracey Addington, Chris Schmidt, John Adcox, and Rick Dunn.

Jack Myers, for his poetry mentorship, and Robert Cochran and Alex Etheridge for their poetry friendship.

My former students at the Hockaday School and Parish Episcopal School, whose examples fill this book, and whose writing taught me even as I taught them.

Everyone at the National Council of Teachers of English for everything they do for English education, for everything their efforts have taught me, and for the opportunity to share my work through articles and through this book. A special thanks to Bonny Graham for her guidance and wisdom throughout this process.

Strike: An Introduction

The best writing lessons and exercises are undoubtedly found in nature and human experience. Poetry is the song of being alive. It is an endlessly optimistic energy of language, and language itself is an energy of existence. It is lightning that arcs from idea to utterance, from flash to resonance. And like lightning, poetry should carry both beauty and danger, form and explosiveness, and should shake us, move us, from the ordinary.

Poets should be moved by other human beings and their voices. They should be moved by the world, by beauty, by suffering. A poet sleeps lightly, or perhaps is even sleepless, for at any moment, the earth may cry out, a crowd may march on a city, a baby babble, leaves or stones tremble, water may rise up against us, a prayer might lift up, a man or woman sing. Experience happens endlessly, and, for poets, the images of experience pass in an endless loop from the world to the imagination to the page and back again. The Romantic poets were moved by nature. But they saw it not simply as something beautiful or as something inspiring but as a spiritual–imaginative force that could dismantle and rebuild the human psyche.

As these experiences enter the mind to become abstract observations and memories, words make them tangible again; likewise for abstract hopes, dreams, fears, the imagination itself. Words flesh out the interior life. Words touch on the location, aims, problems, and triumphs of existence, and though words have serious limits, they still aren't exhausted in their many forms. Words, images, lines, and poems are waiting to be discovered, shaped, and shared.

And in what way should poems be discovered, shaped, and shared? Is there a "way" to write poetry? What is that way, that path? Many workshops and writing texts espouse the craft of writing, a sort of science, if you will. Lightning, too, obviously has its science, but its image and myth remain equal, and its paths branch out in infinite variations and directions. And that is what I hope for this text: that while craft is present, infinite paths open to the writer and the power of the image and the ideas behind myth and myth-making—the power of the imagination itself—remain equally at the heart of the poet's powers. This is the power of creation itself: genesis is not simply the act of creation; it is the joy of it and how it resonates far more deeply and beyond the thing created.

To me, poetry has many powers, many parallels—it is literally a visual embodiment of the human voice, but can contain the voices of animals and insects; the voices of the real and the unreal; the voices of ancestors and of descendants; the voices of those who transcended, those who were vanquished; voices of stone and wind and water. It is the dam and the river. It is a light, a moon reflecting light, a river reflecting light reflected.

In thinking about what these exercises do, I came to the metaphor of lightning late. But once it struck, it clearly fits well with the character and nature of poetry. It is a light in darkness and storm. It is something tangible that seems to form out of nothing, perhaps from the invisible. It moves in all directions in connection with things of a greatly disparate nature. In lightning and in poetry, form and shape are at once definable, yet not predictable. In lightning and poetry: necessity, danger, and thrill. An ability to delight, disturb, disrupt. An ability to transform atmosphere, landscape, and humans themselves. There is heat, height, speed. Sound. Surprise. It is coming around the mountain path into the peaceful valley with a rumble. Poets and nature take raw energy and give it shape, speak it into existence, sometimes a shape so complex that working to understand it can almost never be exhausted. Lightning and poetry give shape to chaos; create and destroy; speak to innocence and experience, heaven and hell. There is thesis and antithesis in lightning and poetry, but it is not just binary. Poetry and lightning both can scatter out into infinite variety, infinite paths, storming above a sea or a volcano or a mind charged with imagination. While lightning can move from cloud to cloud, poetry transmits the feelings of one to the feelings of another. While lightning can move from cloud to ground, poetry can manifest thoughts and ideas into the final shapes of words.

For me, poetry has been a lightning path out of a dark, dangerous place. For me, that place was emotional, psychological, spiritual—as it is with many poets (one of my favorite poets, Franz Wright, comes to mind). For other poets, there is social danger, cultural, even physical, maybe all of the above. For other poets, that lightning path may not be out of or into danger, but into gratitude, maturity, and joy. And for many, writing poetry might be about laying out a path not for themselves, but for others—so voices that have been silenced might be heard.

But don't just wait for inspiration to strike. A poet must learn to create that inspiration, must learn to listen, to work, and to sing. Be like Nikola Tesla—make lightning happen. I trust these exercises will start you on that path—and hopefully carry you far beyond.

The aims of this text are ultimately to inspire, whether that be to inspire a more prescient understanding of the uses of imagery in poetry (to the point of revelation) or to inspire a writer to write more or to write differently or, as may be the case, to write with a new technique or structure. What I might stress most is that though this text does teach technique, technique is never the end goal. A writer undertaking these exercises should never feel a slavish duty to attend to the techniques or "rules." Rather, let the exercise instructions serve as an origin. In this way, the introduction to each exercise, which gives some background to the exercise, what it aims for, and from which poetic/artistic/philosophical question or trend it may have sprung, is just as important as the exercise instruction itself. Likewise, the student examples provided are meant to inspire, to show that each exercise is certainly achievable, and also to celebrate my many wonderful students throughout the years who, parallel to my own reading of poetry, inspired me to teach poetry writing more accurately aimed at what it truly means to be a writer. The student examples herein are not meant to be a quantifiable answer to the question posed. Your poem should not necessarily look like theirs. And though my students pushed themselves to write excellent poetry almost always in accordance with the exercise instructions set forth, indeed you will find examples that deviate slightly from the instructions. Please, feel free. Please, let these exercises launch you into exploration. But, when needed, they can certainly serve as a map as well.

The book as a whole is organized to represent a process through which we discover and navigate the world and poetry itself. First, we encounter the primacy of the image. Before we can think with complexity, we receive sensory input. Thus, the first set of exercises (Chapter 2), "Lightning and Its Shadow: Using and Rethinking Imagery in a Poem," explores the use of imagery in a poem, which is a poem's fundamental way of communicating, just as dialogue is a play's fundamental way of communicating.

Next, as we observe the world and as our brains develop (along with our capacity for language), more complex thought occurs. We ask questions, we learn, we explain, we question again and learn again. And just as this is a greater stage of human development, so too is it a greater aspect of poetry. While the image is the fundamental building block of the poem, the emotional, relational, philosophical, spiritual, or political questions a poem may ask or seek to address are its ultimate aim. Thus, the next chapter, "Cloud to Ground: Using Idea to Manifest a Poem," offers exercises that spring from such questions or encourage writers to ask those questions of themselves. These exercises may ask writers to consider a wide variety of concepts, from the idea of spaces to the nature of games to the structure of their own imagination.

And in human development (or in the development of a landscape or a world), we ultimately come to some sort of shape. Likewise, in poetry, we take our questions and mythologize—that is, give our conceptualized answer. So while Chapter 3 starts writers in the practice of poetically conceptualizing answers to inner (and outer) questions about our world or ourselves, Chapter 4, "Bolt and Arc: Poems That Use and Transcend Form," continues and deepens that practice by presenting exercises about poetic forms that encourage the image (rather than encourage form itself) and structure the development of poetic vision. While poetic forms too often inspire typing, the forms chosen for this text (and the thoughts included in the introductions and instructions) aim toward vision. Included, for example, are Eastern and Middle Eastern forms such as the ghazal and the landay, which are less concerned with rhythm and meter and more interested in the pattern of ideas.

Finally, let this book serve as a point of embarkation. There are so many things, from further information about imagery to writing topics to poetic forms to professional examples, that just wouldn't all fit in this text. So, go and discover, explore, read, experience life, and find your inspiration. For more thoughts on finding inspiration, see the introduction to the "Cloud to Ground: Using Idea to Manifest a Poem" chapter of this book. Go and find the recommended works throughout this book, and through those readings, hear how others experienced life and turned that life into words. And after you have worked through these exercises, and then beyond them, you will, like many writers, find yourself electrifying the atmosphere around you.

Lightning and Its Shadow: Using and Rethinking Imagery in a Poem

Introduction

While I would say that Chapter 3 of this book, "Cloud to Ground: Using Idea to Manifest a Poem," lies at the *heart* of poetry, this section lies at its *fingertips* . . . and in its *eyes* . . . in its *ears* . . . in its *nose* . . . and on its *tongue*. Imagery—the gateway between the world of the mind and the world itself. We touch, smell, see, hear, and taste, taking in the world through these senses, and then processing what we perceive as an image in the brain. Poetry's primary method of communication is the image. Whether it is a simple, single image, two images joined in metaphor or juxtaposition, an epic list, an elaborate exploration of a world teeming with sights and tastes, or the sounds themselves of a line or stanza, a poem's imagery is the brain's companion as it attempts to solve the puzzle of existence. The image serves as an intermediary between the world and the inner self.

There is the image itself and also its implications—"Lightning and Its Shadow," as this chapter's title suggests. A poet presents an image or images but must arrange them, give them context and relationship to other images or to ideas, and must give them a space to exist in our inner lives, whether that be our emotional lives or our philosophical/spiritual lives. The image is the building block, but the image alone does not make the poem—otherwise, a mere list of objects would count as a poem. As writers, we must explore deeper, more complicated ways of considering and using imagery. We must push ourselves to see imagery with fresh eyes, as we did as young children. Albert Camus says that an artist's work "is nothing but this slow trek to rediscover, through the detours of art, those two or three great and simple images in whose presence his heart first opened" (17). And either toward this discovery, or from it, we build more elaborate art that celebrates, explains, mystifies, or even demystifies what we find in the world.

Some of the best scholarship and analysis on how imagery works in poetry can be found in the late Jack Myers's *The Portable Poetry Workshop*. Myers spends a great deal of his text analyzing aspects and types of imagery (surreal, deep, etc.), ways images work with other images (metaphor or juxtaposition), ways imagery moves throughout a poem (centripetal, axial, dendritic, spiral, etc.), and types of poems driven by imagery in different ways (the image narrative, for example). While the exercises in this book do not come directly from Myers's analyses, terms, and categories, they certainly owe his work a huge debt ideologically, as do I personally as a former student of his. His text is highly recommended as an analytical companion piece to these writing exercises.

And much as Myers's text, though analytical in nature, is about the joy of discovering in a poem what one may not have seen previously, these writing exercises are about discovering aspects of imagery not previously perceived, or perhaps about reconnecting with imagery in ways that we once did but have forgotten. Fresh imagery comes from fresh perspective. And much as Myers suggests with his analysis of the movement or shapes of imagery in a poem, several of these exercises encourage writers to track how imagery is a dynamic force in a poem, shifting and transforming, sometimes even into its opposite throughout the course of a lyric.

Recommended Book

Myers, Jack. *The Portable Poetry Workshop*. Heinle Publishers, 2004.

Work Cited

Camus, Albert. Preface. *Lyrical and Critical Essays*. Edited by Philip Thody. Translated by Ellen Conroy Kennedy. Vintage Books, 1970.

Ways of Looking

Wallace Stevens's "Thirteen Ways of Looking at a Blackbird" is one of the most revered poems of the twentieth century. Its imagery and structure capture the dynamic character of nature. An image in a poem is not meant to be a singular, static thing. It is meant to resonate, to reflect, to cast shadows, to leave an imaginative echo in the reader's mind. It is meant to reveal the observations and connections that an author makes and the multiple perspectives that they can hold. This is what makes poetry more than a simple record of things seen. It is a way of seeing. It connects the things seen to the humanness of the seer. Stevens's intentionality in craft—merging form, image, metaphor, diction, perspective— gives his poem an ability to move along with our minds and gives the blackbird an ability to fly off of the page and into our consciousness.

Recommended Poem

Stevens, Wallace. "Thirteen Ways of Looking at a Blackbird." *The Collected Poems*. Vintage Books, 2015. Also found at the Poetry Foundation: www.poetryfoundation.org/poems-and-poets/poems/detail/45236.

The Exercise

Using Wallace Stevens's structure and considering his multiple points of view (both the physical and the metaphysical), write a poem in which thirteen small sections reflect different ways we might see something. Think about how we might see, observe, and understand things beyond merely their immediate visual presence. Some direct description may be involved, but some sections may be a metaphor, some may involve action, some may use setting to reframe the context, some may be spiritual in nature, some may be mundane to capture a portrait of real life, some may take a macroscopic view, and some may take a microscopic view.

Example

Thirteen Ways of Looking at the Early Star of Bethlehem*

I
A Turkish man
gave six yellow blades
to his wife.

II
In a dream,
I was like the stars
for I could see
the other side
and it could see me.

III
Men bruised her skeleton.
Soldiers will eat her seeds.

IV
We swayed like
a single pair
of threaded leaves,

---

*Early Star of Bethlehem is a flower.

lovers laced
in earth.

V
On blue nights,
magicians
practice black
magic.

VI
The Emerald tide is high
yet I can see them
there with the swell,
dancing
without shoes.

VII
His dark aureole.

VIII
As he plucked her,
he mistook
their silky lips
for hers.

IX
Only Wise Men are starry-eyed.

X
Like a heliacal rising,
you stood naked
on the eastern horizon
for only
a brief moment
until
you surged over
the cliff.

XI
As spring began to blossom,
the Early Star of Bethlehem
took a bow.

XII
When the day came,
a slit
between the rays
reminded men
of her
lure.

XIII
Once their eyes drank
her presence,
they galloped away
without
heads
for tears.

—*An Rhiel Wang*

The Image of Time

Time, especially what we perceive to be an image of time, has a complicated relationship to human existence. There are the direct and simple symbols that represent time (a clock, watch, or sundial) and the symbols that easily represent the passing of time (changing seasons). But working past these clichés can open doorways into what time really means to us. Time can reflect abstract things such as our personalities, our fears, our beliefs, and even concrete things such as movement. Doing this well requires subverting the expectations of the reader. Much of time subverts our expectations, even when we should know what is coming—just look at how surprised we are to grow old.

The Exercise

Choose an image related to time to center a poem on. Rather than using an age-old, universal image (such as a clock), think about how an action or movement associated with our modern world might represent time. Particularly think about choosing an image that you feel differently about—maybe one that makes others wistful about the passing of time but that exhilarates you, or vice versa. Around that image, develop other images and commentary about your personality or beliefs that are reflected in that image. Also pay attention to the rhythm of the poem and how carefully placed punctuation and spacing might help the sense of time in the poem.

Example

In this example, notice how what might otherwise be a clichéd image related to time—talking to computer support—becomes fresh. Though it normally carries a negative connotation—one that represents frustration and a waste of time—here Emma uses it to support a virtue that defines her. She furthers that sense of virtue and the image of time in the last three lines, using an unexpected descriptor ("Simple" to describe what otherwise might be wasted "Hours") as well as spacing and punctuation to slow the poem.

Definition

I'm the type of person
who can't pop popcorn—
or compromise—
but loves talking to computer
support line technicians,

being told exactly what to do,
    for infinite.
      Simple.
        Hours.

—*Emma Young*

The Imagery of Body Language

Using the imagery of body language connects the essence of a poem back to something primal in human beings. The movements and sounds of the body were the first language, giving way to more complex forms of expression as spoken, and then written, language developed. Whether in the infant, childhood, adolescent, or adult world, body language remains a defining feature of how humans consciously or unconsciously communicate. We use our hands when we speak. We sit, stand, or walk differently according to our emotions. We let out a cry, sometimes in terror, sometimes in joy, sometimes in sorrow. This kind of imagery is perhaps the most natural way to reflect the deeper emotions of a speaker or character in a piece of writing.

The Exercise

Write a poem in which body language reveals something about a deep emotional or psychological state of a person. You might also consider challenging their gesture or state, possibly even addressing the person directly. To help keep the poem specific and fresh, think about how gestures might connect to the five senses and about the difference between conscious and unconscious gestures.

Example

In this example, a simile comparing a person's sigh to the atmosphere of a restaurant booth (which, in turn, creates some very subtle personification) helps keep the poem fresh. As she addresses and challenges the attitude of her audience, Giovanna goes on to suggest a series of images/gestures that would represent a reversal of the sigh.

You Sigh

You sigh
like an
empty
restaurant booth
once occupied by
    a family of mice
    a sleeping child
    an ancient widow and her driver
but now
now you are pita crumbs and ice chips.
Stand up for yourself!
Comb the scraps from your hair!
Let the amethyst topple
    out of your chest!

—*Giovanna Diaz*

The Imagery of Touch

A poem's foundation is its imagery, and an image's foundation is in the five senses. Because we are predominantly a visual culture, some of the other senses can go neglected. When giving attention to the imagery in a poem, consider how adding one or more of the other senses can give fuller shape to the ideas therein.

Touch in particular opens up many possibilities in adding complicated layers to a poem. Touch involves more than just direct contact, more than just noting that something was touched. When we touch something, we perceive many different things at once. When considering touch, consider concepts such as texture, shape, temperature, weight, movement, pressure, proximity, dullness/ sharpness, and states of matter.

The Exercise
Write a poem in which the sense of touch represents exploring the identity of a person or the nature of an object. Let the imagery of touch grow more complicated through using the different aspects of touch listed in the previous paragraph.

Example
In this example, Katie uses more than one aspect of touch (movement, temperature, texture, and weight) in the first four lines to create the speaker's emotional attitude toward the person in the poem.

Salt

And suddenly I wanted to
run my hands through his cold hair
move the folds in his skin with my fingertips
to feel the weight of his age,
that dark ink line on the X axis.
But I knew he was just a red dot on that map
sometime after the industrial revolution
when they all came
like someone spilled the salt.

—*Katie Bruegger*

Smell and Memory

Of the five senses, it is said that smell has the most direct connection to memory. This makes the imagery of smell a rich mine to draw from in a poem, but it also opens up some dangers. Beginning writers are especially likely to overlook audience as they place an image; and with smell, while it is easy for a writer to drop in the aroma of grandma's cookies, this is not likely to create the same emotional resonance for the reader as for the writer. More work must be done to spell out that connection. In fact, considering the connection between smell and memory itself may be worthwhile. This exercise offers the possibility for that while still maintaining a doorway for personal imagery to enter in.

The Exercise

Write a poem that explores the idea of smell and its connection to memory. This poem may take the shape of a philosophical / physical / metaphysical exploration or it may take the shape of something more personal, wherein specific examples are used to illustrate the connection. Especially if describing smell in general, be sure to use metaphors to help ground smell as an image. Metaphor is an important technique to use here if the direction is more personal, too. Metaphors will help the poem avoid some of the clichéd choices associated with smell (wafting, pungent, sweet, etc.). Consider, too, how smell might be compared to the other senses.

Example

Among other techniques, notice how Brooke's philosophical exploration of the connection uses the sense of touch (line 7) and the sense of taste (line 9) to make smell more active, vibrant, and grounded in something tangible.

Memory, Resurrected

Aromas, incorporeal as shade,
Like fish that gather in an ankle-ring
Which scatter at the slightest motion made,
Confound the tangents of my memory.

Such scents primeval, smoke-like linger, blind,
Above my reach, so graceful, unattached.
Untouched, they press the ceiling of my mind,
To recollections they are never matched.

Sweet clear perfumes that whet my appetite
For long-forgotten days (now fossilized),
Besiege my peace of present, shot mid-flight,
With memories, crypt-ridden, dust-mote-sized.

If ever pinned, these box-less butterflies,
Will raise lost past in gentle sacrifice.

— *Brooke Granowski*

Bittersweet: The Imagery of Taste

Like the sense of touch, there are several facets to the sense of taste. There are five basic "tastes": salty, sour, sweet, bitter, and umami. Beyond that, the imagery of taste may parallel the sense of touch and suggest texture, temperature, and the state of matter (especially liquid or solid). Taste also coincides with quality perhaps much more than any other sense. Something that tastes bad or good evokes a stronger response.

Learning to use imagery well in a poem also means learning that the image itself may be a means to an end rather than an end in and of itself. In this case, for example, what if describing a taste was not your goal, but a way of describing something less tangible? This can be particularly helpful when trying to ground abstract concepts in the real world. Think about the connection between taste and how we describe something emotionally, easily using descriptors like "sweet" or "bittersweet" or phrases like "the taste of victory."

The Exercise
Use the imagery of taste to describe the personal qualities of yourself or someone else. This may involve the actions of the mouth and tongue, the imagery of things that carry a specific taste, or both. Consider the aspects of taste mentioned above to allow a burst of "flavors."

Example

Spiritus Frumenti

sometimes I think your mouth is dry with
sensibilities
and obligations grate on your tongue.
taste the pulsing revivals
the tempered emotions.
maybe you'll need an after-coffee mint.

—*Sarah Harris*

Imagery of the Visual Arts

It makes sense that visual artists who use imagery to reflect human experience would resonate with poets, who seek to do the same through a different medium. Beyond the inspiration itself, much can be learned about technique and the way imagery works in a poem by observing visual arts imagery, by using language to mimic visual arts techniques, and by drawing on the concepts or terms of the visual arts. A perfect example of this is the flying buttress in architecture. The image associated with that term immediately calls to mind a beautiful cathedral and emotionally evokes a vaulting sense of spirituality, all the while reflecting its functional purpose as well. But translating the imagery of one medium to another requires thought. Beyond simply knowing the basic terms and concepts associated with a visual medium, a viewer must begin to understand how style drives differences in the application of those concepts. In other words, not all brushstrokes are the same. A painting by Vincent Van Gogh and one by Salvador Dali would inspire very different feelings through their imagery and their techniques.

Recommended Poem

Auden, W. H. "Musée des Beaux Arts." *Collected Poems*. Vintage Books, 1991.

Recommended Books

Simic, Charles. *Dime-Store Alchemy*. New York Review Book Classics, 2011.

Williams, William Carlos. *Pictures from Brueghel and Other Poems*. New Directions, 1962.

The Exercise

Write a poem that draws upon the imagery of a visual art: architecture, painting, photography, or sculpture. For the purposes of this exercise, you might also consider dance as a visual art. Use the terminology and concepts of that discipline to help give your poem an authentic specificity. You might consider writing directly about a piece of visual art or an artist that inspires you, or you might consider using the imagery of a visual work as a metaphor for something else.

Example

I Am a Body: I Am a Building

I have Frank Lloyd Wright arms today:
Stark fan blades of angled articulation;
Precision found in the whiteness of color.
Line collision tickles my palate
With pigeon wing musculature of stealth,
Streamlined touching.

— *Allison Caldwell*

Imagery of Sound (I Heard Inside)

Imagery in poetry often connects two disparate worlds—the seen and unseen, the inner and outer, the upper and lower. If you think about it, the sense of hearing does this, too. While it may seem like a very external thing, particularly as we focus externally on the sound itself and its source, it actually represents an internal vibration in our ear connecting to something external, or even possibly internal (an animal's voice emanating from inside the throat of the animal, for example). This exercise, which focuses on auditory imagery, encourages the razor-sharp maneuvering needed to explore sounds and connect them to our experience.

The Exercise

Write a poem beginning with the words *I heard inside.* First create the image of what it is that you are hearing inside of, then the images of what those sounds consist of and represent. Think about the various aspects of sound: the scientific properties, such as volume, pitch, timbre, direction, and duration; the social–emotional properties, such as emotion and purpose; and the properties that may cross those categories, such as rhythm. Ultimately, craft images that use sound to create / uncover the mysteries that might lie within something.

Example

Nature

I heard inside
a soft thunderstorm raging from the dirt
the call of a dark fox
tackling the
eclipse screeching above.
They whispered to each other through my silk veins
crying along the pavement of glimmering sorrows.

—*Katie Wall*

Field Recordings

Without a doubt, the best way to find inspiration for a piece of writing is to get out into the world and experience life—meet people, walk through nature, stand in the midst of a chaotic city. But we can't always get out, and sometimes, even when we do, we might find it difficult to take the experience in at the moment or focus on something that would inspire us. I've found that field recordings can be a useful way to find inspiration when you can't get out or perhaps when you find that you get wrapped up in the visual to the neglect of other senses.

When I speak of field recordings here, I don't mean out-of-studio record-ings of music, such as those made by John and Alan Lomax. Field recordings in this sense might be sourced from nature or the city. In them, one might hear the cacophony of taxis, trains, and pedestrians swirling together, or the singular, peaceful flow of a river.

The Exercise

Search online for a field recording, noting as part of your search whether you want to find a natural setting or an urban one. There are many great sources out there. Use the auditory stimulus to help you enter a hyper-focused, hyper-aware, stream-of-consciousness state. Let your writing stream out as a result of the sensory input. Attune to and consider auditory imagery as you write, but let the sounds suggest imagery related to the other senses as well. Think of how the senses might even mix as you write (see the "Synesthesia" exercise in this book for more information on that concept). Most of all, let the sounds take you on a linguistic journey, and write without stopping or worrying about what will come next—go back later and shape the writing as necessary.

Example

city of rain

beyond turnstiles and windmills
she scrubs a rough patch out of the floor

spray paint vigilantes
sing lullabies to trains tucked away in their cement dens

bottles
crushed beneath the glass organs of their friends

everyone
dancing bodies and lights
blurring blobbing
bleeding through the paper
it will be impossible to get home

One time the walking man sign turned on
and I realized I did not turn off the coffee pot

the pieces slip from his fingers
and fall down down through grated vents
sprinkling paper shards on the thick metal skulls.
speeding and screaming away,
they don't even notice.

the rhythmic tapping of suitcase wheels on tile
that would be how a beetle sounds, I should think.

city of rain
another day when the muck and mess
of our shops and schools
spill out onto the streets and
pool into quiet dips in the pavement
like the blood of sacred cows

—*Katharine Lin*

Imagery from Contrasting Music

While a poem lacking imagery runs the greatest risk of failure, even strong imagery can open up new dangers. One such danger arises when writers settle too comfortably into an overly uniform tone. All of the images in the poem seem to fit too nicely together, everything moves in one direction, and we lose the real contrasts, the real conflicts of the world around and within. And while an occasional poem might need to do just that, writers should work to retain the ability to navigate complexity. This exercise will encourage imagery of a dissonant nature—the hard work lies in putting those images together into one piece and maintaining both a contrasting tension and a sense that still those images can work together to say something.

The Exercise
Listen to two pieces of contrasting music (such as Handel versus John Coltrane, Bach versus Thelonious Monk, or Ravi Shankar versus Brian Eno), collecting imagery suggested by each. At first, while listening, just make lists, jot notes, and don't worry about the full, final shape. You might even consider two separate sheets of paper or documents for the imagery that each piece of music suggests. Later, take those images and give careful consideration to what their pairing suggests. Compose a single poem that deals with their dissonant nature.

Example
In this example, the imagery covers a broad spectrum, from tired sitcoms to grieving mothers, from despair to confession. While a reader might not be able to discern much about the two disparate pieces of music that inspired this piece, it is clear that the resulting poem works successfully to craft a single world from extremes.

Emptiness Whistles with Liquid Vengeance

She has the feeling that it will all end like a tired sitcom,
The lights dimming over the familiar furniture against
A final backdrop of fading claps that ask, *please one last chance,*
Knowing the answer will always be no; and fingers will interlace
As the aisles become as empty as the grieving mothers
That find themselves wailing over forgotten
Sons now sleeping behind hollow churches.
And the sound stage will make room for another trite game-show
With a host so tired of his job that the fake smile tearing away
At his face is enough to make the creaking of abandoned houses
Seem like the pleasant banter of barbershop gossip.
Though, in spite of it all she poses
For her pre-paid pictures
With her pre-wrapped lovers
And dances aimlessly while the bartender pours drinks that brag heavily of
    liquor;
And she can almost swear that her own father is sitting
At the end of the long line of albino barstools
Taking sweet bitter shots of memory and wasted love:
This one for the dad daughter dance I traded in for flashing red lights,
This one for going to church as the devil in a three piece suit.
And she will look through the bottom of her glass uttering softly
As if there was a string connecting her can to his;
But the sticky melody of exploding fire hydrants will drench the hall
With smoke and dust—making it a place
Where only wounded soldiers come to pray for absolution,
Drowning out anything but the hymns of redemption
Garnered by the faint glow of Christmas lights hung on July ceilings.
Forgive me Father for I have sinned,
She will whisper into the homeless night,
It has been one forbidden lover and three drinks
Since my last confession.

—Kathleen French

Synesthesia

Imagery is often built from one or more of the five senses, and a poem indeed might use multiple senses to communicate an idea. Synesthesia takes that a step further, however. Synesthesia occurs when the senses are mixed in one moment or experience, for example the idea that a color carries a sound or that a sound could register as a tactile experience. "Mixed" here means more than that they are just used side by side—they are mixed up, as in an experience or observation normally perceived as one sense is perceived by another set of bodily receptors. There are dozens of forms of synesthesia, some as simple as color suggesting taste to as mystical and specific as certain letters or numbers emanating particular colors. This is not just a literary technique. Thought to be a neurological phenomenon, scientists have found that groups of people have at times unconsciously formed similar cross-sensory bonds and entire cultures can share synesthetic beliefs in how they perceive the world. As imagery in a poem, using multiple senses, mixing them, and putting them in surprising contexts (such as using taste as a descriptor for time or place) can produce unusual and stunning, yet subtle, results. The mixture of senses provides an unexpected surprise and helps to jolt the reader out of conscious expectations, thus taking them to a place deeper within or further beyond.

Recommended Poem

Bashō. "The Sea Grows Dark." *The Winged Energy of Delight: Selected Translations*. Translated by Robert Bly. Harper Perennial, 2005.

The Exercise

Write a small poem that uses two to three different senses. Try mixing the senses to create descriptions with a different context. Use taste to describe setting (time or place), or use touch to describe a visual image, or any other combination. Maybe even try ascribing an unusual sense to a person or object. Avoid matching closely linked senses (such as using smell to describe taste or vice versa).

Example

In this example, Katherine uses the simple but surprising descriptor of "sweet and sour" to add a sense of taste to a fall night, creating something at once relatable yet complex and stunningly original.

Arizona

I know you
You're the one
who would drive around with me
on those
sweet and sour
fall nights
while the radio
stumbled over
an infinite playlist

— Katherine Boehrer

The Unexpected Image: Write a Poem about a Tuba

Just as dialogue is foundational to drama, imagery is foundational to poetry. But not all imagery is created equal. What do we do with a basic, mundane, or trivial image? How do we live with it, consider it, react to it, or shape it? Do we leave it as simple or develop it into something full and complex? How will context affect imagery? What image or type/style of image should we use to communicate an idea? The possibilities and choices are near endless, but too often we settle with the first, most basic, most expected image that comes to us—or, as is sometimes the case, settle with the most predictable rendering of that image. Sometimes what we need to work with as a writer is an unexpected image—or an unexpected approach to that image—in order to produce what is truly a poem and not just an observation.

So for this exercise, why a tuba? First and foremost, the tuba seems an incredibly arbitrary possibility for images. A poem about the moon or a tree seems more clear-cut in its possibilities. Second, Morton Marcus's poem "Tuba" serves as a perfect example of how imagery can capture a reader's imagination with its surprise and complexity. Marcus treats the imagery of a tuba, an object many of us might dismiss or find silly, with such dream-like power and reverence.

Recommended Poem

Marcus, Morton. "Tuba." *Origins*. Kayak Books, 1970.

The Exercise

Write a poem about a tuba. Consider what images you will choose, how you will word them, and what context you will give them. Consider purpose. Why would one write a poem about a tuba? How would this affect the imagery of the poem? Could the purpose extend beyond the tuba? Could the tuba become a metaphor for or signifier of something?

Example

In this example, Lily uses the inward and outward flow of air in relation to the tuba and the opening and closing of valves to give the tuba physicality (lung, heart, and brain imagery are all suggested) that is more organic than we might normally think. She also places the speaker in this context (perhaps literally in the tuba) to heighten the emotional intensity.

Organ

Suck me in,
like the blood-air I am.
Into your Prussian valves,
opening and closing
to the time of ill direction.
Then I want to propel from
the bulbous metal cranium,
like an "F" as in "flogging,"
and fly.

—*Lily Simon*

Word as Image

With the rise in popularity of visual forms of texts, such as the graphic novel, there has been much debate about the relationship between words and visual images. But remember that words in and of themselves are images. While some languages are, of course, pictorial in nature, most alphabet and word systems only abstractly represent sounds and ideas. Still, the shapes and even the sounds they represent can carry powerful connotations. And even when plain text is on a plain page, font, size, and spacing can play a powerful role in how we read and understand something. And beyond the pages of a book, the visual impact of words is commanding, whether that be utilitarian (street signs) or expressive (graffiti).

The Exercise

Write a poem in which a word or words—or simply ideas that imply words—are used as images. You might identify the word or words specifically or you might simply invoke a general sense of words as images (for example, by referencing graffiti or skywriting).

Example

Portrait of a Sidewalk in 1992

I wrote my name for the first time
on a sidewalk.

Words like bird, or book, or lemon came later.
Sweet nectar of the alphabet dripped from my palms
into dewy puddles—forming words,
which drowned the hot pavement
like a child's melted popsicle in summer—red, and sticky.

Once, I asked the giving tree
to protect these words from the rain.
To nourish them with soiled water
like she did her children,
the branches and the leaves.
But, they too wilt and die.

—*Alexandra Bishop*

Placing the Abstract in Concrete

Poets have spoken of poetry's ability to make two worlds one. Robert Bly explores it often in both his essays and in his own poetry. His poem "The Third Body" is a fantastic example of how another world exists in the space of the one world we know and experience daily. What exactly is this idea of the two worlds and their becoming one? In her essay "Survival in Two Worlds at Once: Federico García Lorca and Duende," poet Tracy K. Smith says that the struggle of poetry is

> to survive in two worlds at once: the world we see (the one made of people, weather, and hard fact) that, for all its wonders and disappointments, has driven us to the page in the first place; and the world beyond or within this one that, glimpse after glimpse, we attempt to decipher and confirm.

Plato's concept of dualism, and subsequent philosophies such as Gnosticism, tended to separate the physical and spiritual realms, not allowing them to be seen as cohabiting the same space or, at times, having equal value. Interestingly enough, some Christian Gnostics, who eschewed the material world and the body, seemed to miss the fact that when Christ rose from the dead, his body rose and was reclaimed, not merely his spirit. Poetry indeed seeks to join the two worlds—the world of intangibles and ideas and the corporeal world—whether they be the physical and spiritual, body and "mind," actions and emotions, or heaven and earth.

The *words* of ideas are some of the riskiest to include in a poem, for they are often abstractions—words like *love, freedom,* and *happiness.* Writing instruction most often steers writers away from using such words. But what if there was a way to reclaim such words and use them to help reconnect the dual worlds that humans live in? The same goes for imagery that is vague rather than detailed—the default in a writing course is to advise for more description. But what if there was a way to create a more specific context around the image so that it could remain simple? This exercise encourages that idea by having an abstract word placed in a concrete setting. Be sure to read James Wright's "A Breath of Air" for an example of how abstract words and vague images take on concrete forms in the setting and narrative Wright creates.

Recommended Poems

Bly, Robert. "The Third Body." *Eating the Honey of Words: New and Selected Poems*. Harper Perennial, 2000.

Wright, James. "A Breath of Air." *Above the River: The Complete Poems*. Farrar, Straus, and Giroux, 1992.

Recommended Article

Smith, Tracy K. "Survival in Two Worlds at Once: Federico García Lorca and Duende." poets.org. Academy of American Poets, 21 Feb 2005. www.poets.org/poetsorg/text/survival-two-worlds-once-federico-garcia-lorca-and-duende

The Exercise

Choose an abstract, intangible word or idea or a vague image. Put that abstraction in a concrete setting or develop a specific narrative around it to make it seem a physical part of the poem. In some cases, this may result in a sense that the abstraction has been personified or even anthropomorphized, and, in other cases, it may seem part of the physical setting as an object.

Example

In this example by Shaye Martin, she helps give a tangible form to something intangible (dreams) by personifying them and putting them in the context of hospital beds.

Hôpital des Rêves

I rectify my gutted dreams,
    Beheaded and bedridden—
I shall prop them up in their hospital beds.

—Shaye Martin

Characterizing through Inner and Outer Images

In James Wright's poem "The Jewel," he characterizes both his intangible inner self and his tangible inner self (his body) by presenting them as images of the outside world. Wright takes these images a step further than metaphor and, in a softly surreal way, suggests a metamorphosis from one into the other. In other words, his inner nature and his body aren't just *like* something else, they mystically *become* something else. Other poems often do this to help characterize something like the mind or the heart. Much like the exercise "Placing the Abstract in Concrete" in this book, this way of connecting imagery allows for something that is possibly abstract (an inner quality or state of mind) to become tangible. This method could apply to the tangible physical self, too, as Wright does in giving hauntingly beautiful and mystical qualities to his body. Characterizing a speaker or subject in a poem in this way can help reconnect physical imagery to emotions in a surprising way.

Recommended Poem

Wright, James. "The Jewel." *Above the River: The Complete Poems.* Farrar, Straus, and Giroux, 1992.

The Exercise

With the goal of describing yourself or someone else, select three to five images that depict the intangible and/or tangible inner self—anything related to the body or to inner states of mind or heart. For each, develop a corresponding image from the outer world. That corresponding image may just metaphorically reflect the inner body or self—or, in a surreal, dream-like style, it may represent a metaphysical parallel or metamorphosis.

Example

In the example below, to describe her aunt, Emma imagines "disassembling" her face and seeing past tattoos (which seem to be living manifestations of her self) all the way into her lungs and heart, where the imagery of fruit allows us to see that she is "sweet with imperfections." The pairing of fruit imagery (which is easily understood to be "sweet with imperfections") with the imagery of the inner self and the inner body is the perfect pairing to show this idea rather than tell it.

Maria, through the Torn Diamonds of a Broken Chain Link Fence

I focused your eyes
through the robin's
egg glasses,
melting your iron bones
and disassembling your face
so I could gaze
past the atolls
and volcanoes
giving birth to
delicate island chains
that run south
across your bare shoulder
and give way to
the pet tiger
pacing your veldt back.

Then you swung your
ribcage open
just for me.
But your father,
my father's same,
was already there,
picking mangoes
from your lung's
bronchioles
with his long net.
He threw one down
to me, but I dropped it
in favor of your
guava heart,

its tender flesh
so sweet with imperfections.

—*Emma Burke*

Just Because: Using Imagery to Reshape Cause and Effect

Imagery rarely, if ever, stands alone (except perhaps a one-word poem!). Learning to use imagery well often means thinking about the relationship that an image has with other words—and especially the relationship that it has with other images. While two images can have a host of relationships, this exercise focuses on cause and effect to show how a poem can seem to defy logic, yet redeem it through further exploration and showing.

The Exercise

Choose two images that seem illogical if they were to be put into a cause-and-effect relationship, or at least a relationship that would require much further explanation for how the two do reflect cause and effect. Decide on several other images and statements that fill in the gap between their cause and effect. Write the poem, beginning with the word *Because* and letting the cause-and-effect images occupy the first two lines.

Example

In this example, it would seem that the first two lines contain an illogical cause and effect—how could graves make pocket change lose meaning? But the imagery that follows explains that death is the great equalizer, and that, rich or poor, we are all headed to the same place!

Grave

Because our graves are exactly the same size,
Loose pocket change loses meaning.
Nothing more than a child, a household with
Gritty carburetors and rough mechanic hands.
Yellow yachts with platinum bottoms and tigery thrones
Contain no dirty jeans or loose plaid t-shirts.
While golden grocery bags get stuffed with wheat,
Our tombs all have the same letters.

—*Catherine Olivier*

Extended Metaphor

An extended metaphor is one in which a metaphor is described throughout several lines, a stanza, even a full poem (or a paragraph or more in prose). The metaphor generally adds details and possibly even changes a bit as it goes along to represent the dynamic states of the world or of the human mind. A list of *different* metaphors about something does not make an extended metaphor. An extended metaphor could contain multiple instances of figurative language; however, they will revolve around a single theme. Unlike a "layered" metaphor (see the "Layering a Metaphor" exercise in this book for more information), an extended metaphor usually offers a single tenor and a very detailed description of the vehicle. The tenor part of a metaphor is the image that the poet seeks to describe and shed light on. The vehicle is the image that the poet compares the original image (the tenor) to in order to make this happen. The tenor is often physically present in the scene, while the vehicle is often something removed, perhaps imagined, that serves as an imagined parallel.

Recommended Poem

Rumi. "Eating Poetry." *The Winged Energy of Delight: Selected Translations*. Translated by Robert Bly. Harper Perennial, 2005.

The Exercise

Write a poem that is an extended metaphor for one of the following things: your imagination, your face, your sleep, your left foot, Lincoln's beard, the rings of Saturn, a quark, ink, a lost shoe, a jellyfish. Alternatively, you could write a poem that is an extended metaphor for an idea, concept, or discipline: epiphany, mathematics, psychology, advantage, disregard, awareness, routine, unconsciousness, amnesty, or capacity. As you develop the details of the vehicle portion of the metaphor, make use of the five senses as well as other techniques such as synesthesia. Remember, too, that certain details about the vehicle's imagery may deserve their own metaphors as well.

Example

Rhapsody in Blue

Epiphany smells of endless spools
of grosgrain ribbon that live
inside a tuck box that my
elderly neighbor keeps on
her favorite windowsill.

They align themselves by
hue from left to right so
that I can read them like
a love-worn children's book as I
waver between consciences.

The ribbons unfurl—a
rainbowed double-helix behind
vacillating pupils and pulsing corneas.
I realize limits do
not exist when seeping
towards concepts humans have
no ability to grasp.

—*Jordan Naftalis*

Layering a Metaphor

Using an image well in a poem is often about finding connections and making that image a dynamic part of the surrounding world. Poetry is not merely description. As such, while a list or an epic list may be called for at times, imagery in general is not merely a simple record. It must, like an organ, take its place inside a body. While the other parts of the body are quite different, they are connected. Metaphor is an essential technique in allowing imagery to reflect the vibrant expansiveness of the world and offer such connections.

Metaphor itself can be furthered beyond an initial comparison to find multiple connections. Especially with detailed images, metaphors can develop multiple layers, wherein different parts or different aspects of one thing draw several *related* metaphorical comparisons. In this sense, it is important that the metaphors are related or are parts of a whole rather than a list of separate metaphors or one metaphor described in detail, which are different techniques altogether (the latter being an extended metaphor). Unlike extended metaphor, in which the vehicle is usually the detailed portion of the comparison, in layering a metaphor, the tenor *and* vehicle will likely *both* break down into images that contain multiple details (that then align correspondingly). For more information on tenor and vehicle, see the "Extended Metaphor" exercise in this book.

The Exercise
Develop a metaphor in which the tenor portion can be broken down into more than one aspect or detail. Find a vehicle that likewise can be broken down into

the same number of corresponding aspects or details. Create a poem around this relationship. In terms of the mechanics and the musical flow of the poem, it will be helpful to use a variety of figurative techniques (metaphor, simile, personification, hyperbole, etc.) to present the various correspondences between your tenors and vehicles and to use strong sentence variety (phrases and clauses) to help avoid falling into a list-like structure. Complex integration of these ideas into a few sentences will help fuse them together (layer them!) rather than split them apart.

Example

In this example, An Rhiel creates the first layer of metaphor by comparing the wind to a person, then the second layer by comparing the heat of that wind to a "twirling skirt." A third layer is created by seeing this image in full as An Rhiel uses a simile that specifies the person twirling the skirt as a "whirling dervish." There is also perhaps a subtle layer of figurative work that occurs when An Rhiel describes the wind as "yellow." All of that happens in just the five lines of the first stanza! An Rhiel extends that metaphor into the second stanza as well.

At My Old House

Yellow wind
rounds the bend of the creek trees,
twirling his skirt of heat
like a whirling dervish
from Istanbul.

He brushes against the curve of my neck
and my mouth waters
from the taste of the honeysuckles
I used to pick and steal away
to drink behind the bushes.

—An Rhiel Wang

Making a Poem Turn Up or Down

The way a poem ends often leaves a reader with their strongest experience from their reading. Some endings reach full circle, reinforce an idea, ground something in reality, or reveal an epiphany. I've noticed a particular power with poems that "turn up" or "turn down" in their endings—that is, they soar up into images of a spiritual or otherworldly nature to reach some higher level of consciousness, or turn down toward earthly, grounded, realistic imagery to tie the poem more to our bodily life.

"Turn up" ending recommendation: "A Blessing" by James Wright. While Wright spends much of the poem grounded in a very real visual and physical experience (petting horses at the edge of a field), the final three lines turn up to a higher level of consciousness. Wright's poem, even when presenting concrete imagery of the horses, has a very light feeling, but the last three lines vault the poem to a metaphysical level, a spiritual epiphany not obvious from the rest of the poem.

"Turn down" ending recommendation: "Evening Prayer" by Arthur Rimbaud. Rimbaud's poem takes the opposite approach of Wright's, spending most of the poem in a state of reverie and using angelic imagery, but ends with Rimbaud relieving himself after having had too much to drink. As the penultimate stanza gives way to the last, it seems Rimbaud is on the verge of an epiphany like Wright's. But Rimbaud's final image turns decidedly down—not only in its visual sense, but in its essence: the heart of the poem turns down to a very physical, even crude, earth-bound sense of humanity.

Recommended Poems

Rimbaud, Arthur. "Evening Prayer." *Complete Works*. Translated by Paul Schmidt. Harper Perennial, 2008.

Wright, James. "A Blessing." *Above the River: The Complete Poems*. Farrar, Straus, and Giroux, 1992. "A Blessing" can also be found at the Poetry Foundation: www.poetry-foundation.org/poems-and-poets/poems/detail/46481

The Exercise

First, decide whether you want to write a poem that begins in realism and proceeds to the spiritual or metaphysical in its final lines, or a poem that begins by exploring such greater mysteries but ends with a realistic grounding. As the poem reaches its final lines, make the poem turn up or down in its imagery. If the poem is to turn up, make sure to avoid clichéd or vague spiritual aphorisms. If the poem is to turn down, you may want to do as Rimbaud does and create a sort of physical/metaphysical tension, where possibilities give way to reality.

Examples

Turns down: In this example, Madeline begins with imagery that stretches beyond our conscious world, setting her poem in the world of dreams and using soaring imagery such as sails made from skirts and protection magically gained from an "Ottoman hurdy-gurdy." But as these bright, expansive, uplifting images finally meet a sun that offers no sustenance, the poem's imagery crashes back into something much more low, primal, and gastric: those "dreams," or "transcendental cognitions" as she calls them at the end of the poem, must be digested by her liver, so she hopes.

If Scandinavia Could Tell Me Something about Myself

I dream in reservoirs of overlapping images,
where I make lateen sails from my skirts
where lapis and dereliction are not fungible commodities
and insanity is insatiable
an Ottoman hurdy-gurdy waxes my knees
with rosined bow strikes
to protect them from
Cassandra's
orations, like a potpourri orange sun
from which I can suck no juice
Only I wonder, might I chew the rind
and hope to digest transcendental cognition
with my liver?

—*Madeline Burch*

Turns up: In this example, Caitlyn spends much of the poem building imagery around a typical Sunday morning at home: coffee, spoons, Sunday paper, etc. The images are detailed, rich, interesting, and some are literal, while others utilize figurative language. But the poem's purpose is not merely to record the details of a Sunday morning. Ultimately, Caitlyn wants the reader to experience the transcendent rapture of such moments. Thus, just when it seems that the poem has broken down into a list (sugar, milk, and mail), it actually uses these images to launch into a moment of otherworldly beauty, one represented by a sublime, imaginative image: "a diamond beneath your skin."

I Speak Another Language

Instant-coffee perfume and the
ring of spoons against porcelain cups
tell me it's morning.
Your feet shuffle on white carpet as
slumbering daylight pools at the
window frames.

Here is the Sunday paper.
When you open the shutters, crumbs of
dust glow under yellow strands as I
wash the dishes at the sink
to the hum of talk radio.
One sugar, a tablespoon of milk,
my name scrawled across the envelopes
of already-opened mail.
At daybreak the sunlight always reminds me
there's a diamond beneath your skin.

—*Caitlyn Le*

Transcendental Imagery

In the "Making a Poem Turn Up or Down" exercise, I introduced the idea that a poem could proceed mostly in grounded, realistic imagery and end with an epiphany or a transcendental moment—or vice versa. But this idea of transcendental imagery need not be relegated to the end of a poem. Using such a technique at the end makes for a wholly different experience—one in which the reader understands just as much about the nature of epiphany or transcendence as the subject at hand. But if the transcendental imagery is spread throughout the poem, or perhaps at least used midway, the focus then lies much more with the subject itself.

The Exercise

Write a poem about a person so inspiring, interesting, or beautiful that they seem to transcend reality. Let the entire poem focus on the transcendence. Make sure to use concrete imagery, but let that imagery be pulled into an "upper" atmosphere (a dream world, a heaven, infinity, etc.).

Example

Newspaper

And one day in the morning,
with twigs and sun in your hair,
and your sister in the kitchen,

you'll just go on forever that way—
with your eyelashes and sandals

and not even a newspaper
could capture your bare foot
and pull it back down.

—Lilly Lerer

Shifting Image

Poetic imagery, not meant to be a still life, isn't often static. Sometimes the image finds dynamism in its relationship to other images. At other times, an image itself is dynamic and "shifts" through different states or stages. An image can begin to change over the course of a few lines or a whole poem. It can morph quickly or slowly, experience a radical shift, jump, or leap, it can shatter into something else, it can even experience a change when controlled or viewed through a specific lens (such as the author's preconceived notions or a particular level of consciousness, or perhaps even a lens unrelated to the author, such as through a shift in perspective), and can seem to reflect a wholly new image when viewed from a different angle or a shifting mode of thought. A seed becomes a tree, or vice versa if this is viewed in reverse.

An image might shift due to age, size, appearance, style, purpose, state of matter, changing emotional states, changing states of consciousness, shifting perspectives or contexts, or through many other means. Often these shifts are gradual or represent small or incremental changes and are not necessarily represented by extremes. Think about aging: a shift from young to old does not happen overnight. Exploring a shifting image does not necessarily mean that a writer is interested in extremes. While old might be the extreme opposite of young, a writer might be more interested in the subtle shift from childhood to young adulthood, which are not opposites. Images can indeed shift from one extreme to another (essentially turning something into its own opposite), but the application of that use of imagery would be so different that I have included it as a separate exercise, "Enantiodromia."

Recommended Poems

Myers, Jack. "Doing and Being: A Story about the Buddha." *One on One*. Autumn House Press, 1999. In addition to looking at the "shifting" progress of Buddha himself, Myers's poem also contains the fantastic image of a mountain being worn down by way of a raven dragging a scarf over the mountaintop once every hundred years.

Tate, James. "First Lesson." *Selected Poems*. Wesleyan, 1991. A very different kind of "shifting poem," James Tate's "First Lesson" shifts an image of a snake with legs first through slight, and then great, alterations to teach us a lesson about how not to meditate.

The Exercise
Write a poem in which an image changes over the course of the poem. Rather than focusing on the extremes of the first and last or before and after, think about placing the focus on the shift itself—the minute details that happen in between stages or over a period of time or a range in size or in a shift from wakefulness to sleep, etc. Use additional imagery to detail the process of the original shifting image.

Example
In the following example, Kristin explores the shift in her "consciousness" (from awake to "unconscious"/asleep) during biology class, using the timely metaphor of prometaphase.

dozing off

biology may be the
study of (my) life,
but it is also my
worst
subject.
I sit in the
classroom and the
teacher explains that
     "in prometaphase, the
      nuclear envelope
      begins to
       disintegrate"

(quite coincidentally) my own yarn consciousness, a tangle of
chromosomal thoughts breaks into prometaphase—right then!
and my lab desk, the deep onyx slab, melts into the vacuum of a child's closet
   where
after finding the perfect hiding spot I can see the burns in my corneas, sharp
   sparks like
the grains of sand I felt under my neck three years ago when I sprawled across
   an unproviding

beach towel and found that the cotton loops curve just like contoured Matisse
   sketches on cursory paper in too-cautious museums that protect against
   mustached robbers and
overassuming analysts who look to art for explanation of a physical existence,
   asking their neighbors—

"ARE YOU AWAKE?"

—in the way my
biology teacher is
asking me a
      second
after I realize that
I am sitting
in my classroom

mouth agape in slumber
or perhaps at my sudden
understanding of
prometaphase.

—*Kristin Lin*

Lilly Lerer's poem "Hey Kurt," included as an example for the "Reclaiming Our
Environment" exercise in Chapter 3, also shifts, but does so backwards.

Enantiodromia

Enantiodromia refers to the changing of something into its opposite. It comes
from a Greek concept (*enantios*, opposite + *dromos*, running course) but was more
recently popularized by Carl Jung, who thought of it as the overabundance
of a force eventually turning into its opposite. In psychology it could refer to
the unconscious acting against the wishes of the conscious, and in the natural
world could be thought of as a principle of equilibrium. Much like the "Shifting
Image" exercise, this exercise asks the writer to consider the change in an image
over the course of a poem, but whereas a shifting image could shift slightly or
into a marginally altered state, this exercise encourages a more exact turning
into a complete opposite.

The Exercise

Write a poem in which one object or idea turns into its opposite. Develop imagery primarily around the two extremes: the beginning and end, first and last, before and after, the different sizes, shapes, states, etc. Think about what placing those extremes side by side tells us about their nature and the nature of the world, much as you would do with juxtaposition. Juxtaposition would be a perfect technique to use in this exercise, but even if not used directly, the reader should finish the poem with a clear sense of the two opposites side by side.

As an alternate exercise, write a poem in which two opposites work together (work together in their contrasting forces) to produce a new, third thing.

Example

The Principle

The pleasure to finish becomes
the agony of starting.

The pleasure to start meets
the agony of finishing.

—*Jovan Hill*

Epistrophy

I'll bet you never thought of jazz and the plant world as having much in common. But in truth, many parallels can be found in their patterns, their "improvisations," their transformations, their rhythms. This exercise is inspired by a song by Thelonious Monk, "Epistrophy," and by that word's meaning in the world of botany. In botany, *epistrophy* refers to the reversion of an abnormal form or type to the normal. This term as used in botany actually comes from a philosophical term (*epistrophe*), which is a doctrine addressing the return of all intelligence by a law of nature to the divine center. Thelonious Monk's "Epistrophy" works in much the same way as described by these terms, beginning with an odd-sounding blast of notes, chords that are a semitone apart, and then returning to a more standard melody. Writing with this pattern in mind, the writer can gain from this exercise a greater sense of control between the abstract and the concrete, the figurative and the literal, and the avant-garde and the straightforward.

The Exercise

Write a poem in which a first stanza, movement, or section communicates an idea with fragmentation, figurative language, and avant-garde or surreal associations. The second stanza, movement, or section should continue that same idea in a concrete, straightforward, reflective way, but should not attempt to decode the first part; rather, it should simply add to it in a more direct, accessible way. Think about how, even though the style is simpler in the second part, the additional imagery and commentary complicates the first part—in other words, might you be risking something by saying it plainly?

Example

I Do Believe

Let me reach between your collar bones,
where your chest burrows
and I may grope for the
conundrum that you called soul,
where galaxies drip into your gut
like a memory on
braided wick.
Then, grotesque, I
move.

I should not have yelled
when you harangued me with your
righteousness.
Instead,
I should have leaned out the window
into the salty breeze
and baptized myself
in silence.

—*Madeline Burch*

Cloud to Ground: Using Idea to Manifest a Poem

Introduction

In just my second year teaching a full Creative Writing course, I realized that I was spending as much time addressing *what* to write as *how* to write. Students had writer's block; they "didn't have anything exciting to write about"; when uninspired students did pick an "exciting topic," it seemed to be the time they scored the winning goal (a losing topic, for sure). While the exercises in this section of the book will immediately give many topics to choose from, most of all, I hope that they reconnect writers to the literally infinite possibilities for ideas out there in the world. Whenever I tell someone that I am a poet, there is one surefire way that I can tell if they know nothing about poetry—if they then ask me, "Oh, what do you write about?" Poetry is about everything.

Imagery is the foundational element of a poem, and an image absolutely can be the sparking genesis of a poem, but, at times, the idea comes first, and the images follow. Philosophy, theology, our libraries, cartoons, games, mathematics, personal loss, the visual arts, epic journeys, pollution, trinkets, space—there is no territory that is untouched by imagery, and thus, untouched by poetry. These disciplines, ideas, experiences, rituals, questions, people, cultures, events, and objects are waiting to be explored in verse.

Beyond these writing exercises, which will shed more specific light on exploring many of these areas, I say get up and go out and find your inspiration. Inspiration can come from a variety of sources. Federico García Lorca describes it as duende, a devilish spirit that resides within the author and manifests itself in an earthy way. Ed Hirsch, Rainer Maria Rilke, and others describe inspiration from the reverse vantage point: the angel, an outward and heavenly source of inspiration. In many ways, both of these are true, but how do they operate? Can one access them? Must one wait to be moved by the duende or the angel?

A writer does not often have time to sit idly and let inspiration magically happen. A writer must often act to make inspiration happen—again, like Tesla: make the lightning. You must get up and get away from your computer. Inspiration isn't likely to strike as you watch the cursor blink.

Get up and go out. Go out at midnight. Go out in the afternoon and demand to hear a stranger's story. Get on a bus. Demand to tell your story to a stranger. Demand to tell your story to a friend—better yet, an estranged friend, making yourself familiar again. Involve yourself.

Talk to yourself. Out loud. Pace around while you do this. Get louder. Scream. Get angry if you have to, but practice peace and repentance, too. Sit in silence. Shut the mind's mouth from moving and let the world pour in (as in certain types of meditation).

Listen. Listen to the quiet, the loud, the hysterical, the hilarious. Listen to people—eavesdrop. People watch. Snoop. Get jealous—over a person, a poem, a painting, a photograph, a sound. Listen to something crazy—whether it be music (instrumental) or the voices in your head. Make sounds—weird poetry sounds—out loud. Do it for real. Listen to yourself making sounds. Listen to the night. Be jealous of its immensity.

Stay up late. Type nonsense at 1 a.m. and decode it at 10:00 a.m. Drink lots of tea and coffee. Get some rest if you need to. Sleep and write your masterpiece while you're dreaming or when you wake up in the middle of the night. Keep a pen and paper by your bed. In fact, keep a pen with you at all times. Write your masterpiece on napkins.

Sit by yourself at lunch and doodle and write on napkins or in notebooks. Be weird like this and enjoy it. Be nutty and quirky. Act absurdly, in the spirit of the wise, all-knowing fool. Try on a persona—or recognize that you are one, or two, or ten. Tell the truth—even if it's about how you're lying. If this doesn't seem to work, stop—stomp around the room, and demand.

Stop trying to impress or trying to be correct or trying to be like a student trying to be better—be a vulnerable and confident, passionate and compassionate, fierce human being. Be fierce—a fierce humanitarian and voice for humans. Stop being so polite—not in order to be rude, but in order to speak up and let yourself be heard and the concerns of others be heard. Write your life and all the life around you.

The Imagination: From an Intangible Form to a Tangible One

Our imagination, language, the images we carry, the visions we dream all reside somewhere almost intangible until we perform the act necessary to make them presentable to an audience (we write, dance, paint so that others can see our inner lives). That is what art often is: making the intangible tangible. Even in painting a still life, a painter is not seeking merely to copy the externals of that tangible thing before him, but wants to get at its inner life. Understanding the connection and relationship between the intangible and tangible helps artists understand consciousness and how it plays a role not only in art, but also in our lives as sentient beings. Robert Bly's wonderful anthology *News of the Universe: Poems of Twofold Consciousness* collects poems that work on multiple levels of consciousness at once. The poems therein are expert examples of when the ordinary and extraordinary collide, employing what Bly refers to as "leaping" imagery that can communicate between and even merge what we sometimes perceive as disparate levels of being: the tangible/intangible, conscious/subconscious, the body/the spiritual.

When young writers struggle with a piece they are writing, it seems they have trouble not only in communicating with others, but also in communicating with themselves. They tend to get stuck in one frame of reference, whether it be an overly literal vision of the world or a head-in-the-clouds aloofness. The parts of their consciousness can't talk back and forth, and they may even be unaware of certain parts of their consciousness (the subconscious, for example). In fact, young writers may not even know they are stuck in their writing at all: for unfortunately in our culture today, competency is king rather than surprise or ingenuity.

A variety of exercises and methods can help writers more readily access other levels of consciousness as they write: music, meditation, steam-of-consciousness writing. Ultimately, the goal of such methods is to bridge a gap between states of mind, therein establishing a more enlightened sense of the world. Understanding the relationship that an artist's own inner life has to the external world is a great way for them to become self-aware in many respects. This exercise helps to bridge the gap between that intangible place where art is born and the tangible life it has on the page, stage, or canvas. Thinking and writing about the process of the genesis of an idea to its physical formation can help us more easily access that unconscious or subconscious level that our imaginations often reside in.

Recommended Book

Bly, Robert, editor. *News of the Universe: Poems of Twofold Consciousness.* Counterpoint, 2015.

The Exercise

Imagine where your storehouse of words and imaginative ideas (your images, your movements for dance, your lines when you paint) exist. This might be an inner place such as your mind or heart or gut, or it might be an outer place such as the sky or in a dictionary. It might even be a spiritual or imaginary place, such as in the palm of God's hand or in imaginary boxes. It might even reside some-where between, such as in your dreams while asleep. Once you've determined a place that your words and imaginative ideas reside, visualize what happens as those become real, as they go from that place where they live to their home on the page. Does your body involve itself in the act of writing? Is there some-thing that translates or transforms or carries or converts the words and ideas? Do they appear somehow in a mystical way? Write a poem using a variety of imagery and figurative language to describe what that is like: creating setting, seeing yourself and maybe even these words and ideas as characters, narrating the process of those words and ideas coming out.

Example

In this example, An Rhiel draws upon the mythology of the *Ramayana* and frames the process of her imagination becoming tangible within the metaphor of Sita's vulnerability at the hands of Ravana. It is both a tender and a powerful reminder of the imagination's ability to transform, even sometimes in a way that threatens us.

Ravana

I break from the ring
so carefully drawn by Rama's aureate arrow
in a labyrinth of peat moss and vines
to suffer the fire
kindled by titian silk
and tended by demon beast, Ravana.

His thirst for terror
blackens the night that blankets my body
convulsed and writhed
of virulent venom.

So I break from flesh
to rise like smoke
and stain like charcoal
against the callous of his hands.

—*An Rhiel Wang*

Firsts

In the language arts, poetry is the perfect medium to capture a small, but powerful, moment. And what moment would be more powerful than a first? Experience is the best teacher, and the first experience with something, good or bad, leaves impressions like lightning, striking and branching out in connection. In fact, this is how the brain learns. The first time we are exposed to something, whether it be something visual or an experience or an idea, our brain seeks to connect it to something that we already know, have observed, or have experienced.

The Exercise

Write a poem about a "first": a kiss, a cartwheel, an encounter with the police, a paycheck, a "coming of age" moment, a camera, falling off a bicycle, driving a car, failing a test, seeing the ocean, eating sushi, tying your shoe, seeing something triumphant or tragic live on the news—anything that was significant to you as a first—good or bad. Some "firsts" are a bit tired and might run the risks of cliché—the first day of school, for example. Whatever subject you choose, be sure to employ the various techniques related to creating fresh imagery from the imagery chapter of this book. Let the images show the feeling of the moment rather than telling it explicitly.

Example

Greener

It is a green shorts summer,
when I cartwheel across the grass
for the first time ever.
Letting pine needles stick to my palms,
And dirt stain my skin,
forgetting with every cartwheel,
the falls, and
accidental tumbles.
Hand over hand,
feet in the air.
The crown of ferns on my head
falls to the ground.

—*Emily Nielson*

Space

We often concern ourselves with what is present, but it can be important to question what is not there—and important to even see what is not there as something. Space—a nothing that is something. Think of space in all its forms—outer space, the space between things, inner space, silence, nothingness, the space between moments.

The Exercise

Write a poem about what you do or would do with space/spaces. Do you fill them? With what? Increase them, filling space with more space—for instance, offering up a silence in response to silence? Do you relish spaces or fear them?

You could also create a narrative poem in which a character deals with spaces in an unusual way. For instance, rethink what it means to hoard. We think of hoarders as needing (or thinking they need) a great number of material things—what if they are really just filling up spaces, needing an obliteration of space?

Whatever form you choose, collect/create tangible imagery and get down to the root of things—motives and results.

Example

Please

Please,
take care
as I lead you through the lemon trees!
For I am partial
to letting the limber branches whip back
to fill the space between us.
The leaves swatting at your eyelashes –
the legs of two fat, slumbering flies
peeking out from under their covers.

—*Giovanna Diaz*

The Invisible

The concept of invisibility fits well into the world of poetry, for it so easily evokes mystery and ambiguity. Some possible fresh angles here include choosing an imagined, invisible object to represent a state of mind, as Robert Bly and Kay Ryan do in the recommended poems below.

Unlike the previous exercise "Space," which explores the idea of nothingness, the concept of invisibility suggests a something, though not seen or not present. Whether applied to a person or an object, invisibility can open a door to explore a number of other concepts: identity, human relationships, the nature of material or spirit. The concept might be applied through science fiction, but poetry also allows for surreal imagery, or even simply metaphor, to anchor the poem in a more familiar world.

Recommended Poems

Bly, Robert. "My Father's Wedding." *The Man in the Black Coat Turns*. Harper Perennial, 1988.

Ryan, Kay. "Carrying a Ladder." *The Niagara River*. Grove Press, 2005. Ryan's poem can also be found at the Poetry Foundation: www.poetryfoundation.org/poetrymagazine/poems/detail/42132

The Exercise

Write a poem about the invisible, especially something specific that is or becomes invisible. Some different directions to consider: things that are normally visible that could be invisible in a given context; the process by which something becomes invisible; invisibility as a metaphor; various states and degrees of invisibility; invisibility as a measure of another force or action.

Example

Ironwood Dreams

Driving up to
the top of the ridge that day,
light through the holes
in the roof of the Oldsmobile
cuts constellations across your cheeks,
and blossoms from shower trees
slipped through cracked windows.
But as they fell they covered your face
and bit by bit,
eye by nose,
you disappeared.

—*Emma Burke*

Epic Journey

The epic journey was, of course, historically one of the standards of literature, the subject of the epic poems. But I think we can capture something of the epic journey in a different way now, through a shorter treatment. A smaller poem can leave a more selective group of images to resonate in the reader while still capturing the expansiveness of the epic journey.

The Exercise

Write a short poem that details someone's epic journey. Think of using imagery (such as natural or cosmic imagery) that, even while specific, could evoke something grand, sweeping, and powerful.

Example

From Southern China to India: My Grandfather's Journey

The Gooney Bird vexes like demons the sky:
a DC3 monster
—unrefined and metal—
grinds his jaw,
rattling valor like chains.

He swallows twenty-eight souls whole;
their bodies eat away at sanity,
leaving them to dine
on little oxygen and dementia.

Twenty thousand feet:
where sleeted veins
of the Himalayan Mountains
protrude,
breathing is a daft attempt—
so the DC3 dares his captives
hold their breath
as he cackles starless smoke.

Upon landing,
he vomits people who walk away
a godsend.

—An Rhiel Wang

Game/Event Poem

Writers have chosen many forms to explore the idea of ritual, game playing, and superstition. Some have written fiction; Richard Connell's "The Most Dangerous Game" puts an interesting twist on the sport of hunting. And others, nonfiction or poetry. Certainly many an essay has been written exploring games, which can often become ritualistic in and of themselves, as well as other ritualistic events.

Game, or event, "poems" are records of rituals often from, but not restricted to, tribal cultures. Jerome Rothenberg has collected a fantastic set of these poems (which are adapted from folk literature, scripture, records of shamans and tribal customs) in his anthology *Technicians of the Sacred*. These writings help capture the beautiful and sometimes odd response of humans to the world around them (whether that be a primitive or a modern world), to other people, to culture, and to themselves. They could emanate from old wives' tales, from religious ceremonies, cultural or personal rituals, or (in our modern world) our phobias and paranoias. The game/event poems in *Technicians of the Sacred* draw a close parallel between games and cultural rituals and superstitions. This connection easily makes sense if you think about certain games in particular: ring around the rosie, chess, chase/tag, even Monopoly! The same might be seen in our rituals, superstitions, and celebrations: think about how they represent the "game" of life!

Recommended Poems

Simic, Charles. "Evening Chess." *Hotel Insomnia*. Harcourt Brace, 1992.

Simic, Charles. "Prodigy." *Selected Early Poems*. George Braziller, 2013. "Prodigy" is also available at poets.org: www.poets.org/poetsorg/poem/prodigy

Recommended Books

Popa, Vasko. *Homage to the Lame Wolf*. Oberlin College Press, 1987. Popa's book features an entire section on games, including such poems as "Before the Game," "Hide-And-Seek," "Between Games," and "After Play."

Rothenberg, Jerome, editor. *Technicians of the Sacred: A Range of Poetries from Africa, America, Asia, Europe, & Oceania*. University of California Press, 1985.

The Exercise

Write a lyric, narrative, or list poem about a game or cultural event. Some possible topics: any type of game, a sport, a ritual, a religious rite, a superstition, a celebration.

Example

In this example, Emily writes a narrative poem about playing hide-and-seek in the woods behind her grandfather's house. Setting plays a large role in hide-and-seek, so Emily gives great attention to those images. It being a narrative poem, she also gives subtle, but important, details about herself, her sister, and her grandfather. Also notice Emily's excellent choices in terms of sentence style and line breaks.

Hide and Seek

Underfoot, pine needles
and acorn top hats,
ground, damp from melted
snow. Overhead,
light pulses through tree branches.
These trees are older than the rings around their
trunk say they are.
I tug at my sister's hand,
driven deeper into the woods,
where leaves are changing,
originally heavy with snow, now,
crisp and regrown.
My eyes on a birch far ahead,
its dead bark curling
and crunched. The perfect hiding spot.
But Grandpa, who knows the forest better,
finds us.
Success.
I find freedom in the forest
behind Grandpa's house,
but the canopy always hung above us.
Watching.

—Emily Nielson

Cards

This exercise is closely related to the "Game/Event Poem," but looks at playing cards specifically. Cards and card games are worth their own look as they contain such rich visuals, characters, and even the possibility of narratives, whether those are narratives that play out between the cards themselves or between people playing cards. Cards and card games have inspired or played a role in much great fiction; it is time for poets to get in the game!

The Exercises

This topic suggests many possible exercises—perhaps as many permutations as a deck of cards itself.

1. Write a poem about one card from a deck of playing cards. Instead of merely describing the card, think about what the card suggests metaphorically or what the inner life of that card personified might be. A lyrical poem celebrating the colors and shapes of the card might be in order, but so might a narrative poem. Don't be tempted to only choose one of the character cards (king, queen, jack, joker). For example, if you picked the two of diamonds, what would two of diamonds, personified, be like?

2. Choose two cards from a deck and write a poem about what might happen when these two cards come together. Would you personify them and create a narrative poem? Would a narrative poem develop out of what might happen if someone drew these two cards in a poker game?

3. Write a poem about the design on the back of the card. When we think of cards, we often think of the face, but in a card game, it is the intricate but mysterious design on the back of the card that most perplexes us as we wonder what lies in our opponent's hand!

4. Write a poem about a specific card game (solitaire, poker, gin, spades, etc.). The poem could be a lyric exploration of the psychology of the game; the game could serve as a metaphor for something else; or you might write a narrative poem about people playing a specific card game. Consider using the imagery of one or more specific cards as you develop the imagery of the game.

5. Write a poem about a magic trick involving a deck of cards.

6. This exercise would be great for a group writing together—a creative writing class or a workshop. Deal out separate cards to each person in the group. Then, each person writes a poem for their card. From there, some other possibilities for the group: share the poems without indicating which card was the subject of the poem (some poems might easily and directly identify the card even without an identifying title, but others might require some interpretation); if you have enough people in the group or enough time to write poems for each card in a deck, the group could try to play a card game using the poems instead of the deck itself.

Example

King of Spades

His sleepy Majesty, the
Insomnia-addict king,
Saw his royal eyes spinning toward
A relic's royal scars,
Drunk in his exhaustion
And marveled at the sword,
Official royal wishing:
He knew who to use it for.

—Ellie Munson

Trinket Poem

In the twentieth century, a quiet, reclusive man named Joseph Cornell gained fame as an artist through his assemblage of found objects in shadow boxes. Through his careful arrangement of eclectic material, Cornell elevated what otherwise may have been thrown away or overlooked at a secondhand shop to an image that should move and be treasured by the viewer. Cornell's boxes are filled with soap bubble pipes, doll heads, paper birds, glass jars, marbles, and many other trinkets, but, assembled with aesthetic purpose, they carry weight. While nostalgia was certainly a feeling sometimes evoked by these boxes, Cornell was just as easily able to evoke fear, sorrow, or spiritual enlightenment. While Cornell was clearly influenced by the surrealists and dadaists, he achieved something very different from what they did. While Duchamp elevated the urinal to the status of a work of art, he did so just as much to make a comment about art. In Cornell's work, he did so to, as he stated, create "white magic" rather than "black magic."

Recommended Books

Foer, Jonathan Safran, editor. *A Convergence of Birds: Original Fiction and Poetry Inspired by Joseph Cornell*. Distributed Art Publishers, 2001. Foer's anthology features work by poets and prose writers who were inspired by Cornell.

Simic, Charles. *Dime-Store Alchemy: The Art of Joseph Cornell*. New York Review Books, 2011. Inspired by Cornell's work, the poet Charles Simic wrote this entire book of prose poems based on some of the shadow boxes. (Also recommended for the "Imagery of the Visual Arts" exercise in Chapter 2.)

The Exercise

Find a trinket, maybe one around your house or one from a thrift store . . . or, have someone supply you with a trinket or a choice of several trinkets. Think of the kind of cheap things a child might collect: pencil toppers, a fake ring, a rubber lizard or snake, a button, a cheap figurine, a green army man, a souvenir coin, a key chain, miniature cars or food items, toy airplanes, kazoos, marbles, dice, fortune from a fortune cookie, an old key, etc.

Write a poem that celebrates the trinket, describing it, but even more so connecting it with stories and images from beyond the immediate. While odes may be about the stars or the trees or the mountains, they could also certainly be about a trinket. Thinking of this poem as an ode is especially important, since the goal is to bring honor to something that otherwise might have little value.

Example

This example by Alex Edwards was inspired by a rabbit's foot.

A Fluke

As the grass moaned and the birds followed,
The shotgun prisoned the rabbit

I cut off one leg
Soundless
The rabbit stared at me
With hungry eyes

—*Alex Edwards*

What's in a Filing Cabinet?

This exercise can help a writer to plumb the unseen and to experiment with different forms. That which is secretive, that which is a mystery, always stimulates the imagination. You must see past the filing cabinet and build something from your imagination. The filing cabinet itself may or may not be important—but that which is within bursts through the doors and drawers of the cabinet with imagery and story.

The Exercise

Write a poem that reveals what might be hidden in a filing cabinet. Such a poem might describe a legal brief, tax returns, old photographs, even a bottle of whiskey. You might write about something hidden in a metaphorical sense. If what is hidden is a poem itself, you might consider re-creating it as the hidden document: think about what kind of poem might be hidden, locked, or filed away for future reference. Also consider the possibilities of form here: maybe the poem comes in the form of a letter, includes visual elements, or is composed of mysterious fragments, though of course a lyric or narrative poem would also certainly be appropriate.

Example

Filed After Z

Engraved in this manila folder
are your whispers:
the perforations of picture shows
and the creases of your poetry slumbers.
And I have filed them all amongst
the metallic oblivion of
phone bills and rejection letters
to be sought in the
pauses between
contentments.

—*Audrey Baker*

Manufactured Landscape

"Nature" poems have often looked to the natural world for humans to find inspiration. But our modern environments are increasingly human-made, manufactured and "unnatural." Still, these objects (buildings, cars, concrete, cellphone towers, glass, metal, furniture, electronics, etc.) can shape our psyche, can seem to contain a consciousness (even if it be a lower one) just as the natural world can. It's also interesting to note how nature itself can be shaped and manufactured and become part of our modern, human-made landscapes. This can have results that are beautiful (human-made lakes), colossal (dams), hilarious (bushes sculpted to look like figures), meditative (bonsai), or aesthetically tragic (trees butchered into deformation to protect power lines). Sometimes, as with faux wood, we even manufacture something to replicate nature, or try to control nature as if it were a product, or try to join the world of architecture and nature together in a harmonious way, as with a tree house.

The Exercise

Write an "unnatural" nature piece, that is, a piece of writing that uses human-made objects as an environment or force that drives the psychology/philosophy of the writing . . . or a piece in which humans treat nature in that unnatural, objectified way. Let the environment, landscape, or objects interact with humans in some way. Try to understand both the consciousness (the internal, emotional qualities) of the human-made things and the consciousness of the human being, merging them, if possible.

Example

woodcut

she chokes the forest with her hand.
a hold of four strings and a grasp around the neck,
slapping her hand.
keeping her hold like a dead chicken.
when she is not playing, she lets the trees move.
with the placement of her fingers
and the release of the carved grain,
the tears of bears flood the cabin.

— *Ash Chen*

Earth in Transformation

The movie *Powaqqatsi* shows in its first half the world of hard labor, crude tools, and humans working in a natural setting. Midway, it then jumps quite abruptly into the world of artifice and technology (trains, cars, advertisements). There is still a hardness about life and work—children bearing loads of tinder become children bearing bundles of tires, and so on. The images offer a context for us to properly view our advances and our limits rather than simply seeing everything as progress.

This exercise requires you to do something twofold: write about something physical, and consider the transformation or transition of that thing (whether it be an object, idea, person, an act, etc.) from one state to another.

The Exercise

Using the imagery of the earth, imagery of work, and imagery of machines and tools (both crude and refined), write about some sort of transition or transformation. Think of the prefix *-trans* and all of its associated words and their subtle meanings: *transubstantiation, transpire, transmit, transducer, transcend, transmute,* and others. Think about whether one of these and its subtleties would best be applied to what you wish to write about. Also decide if your transition/transformation is a slow one, or is abrupt, or something else entirely.

For the imagery, you can use these images in an extended metaphor, in a series of brief metaphors, in a literal way, or in any combination of these methods. Avoid overly heavy or tired symbolism such as the changing seasons. The earth images do not necessarily have to turn into images of machinery . . . these images could be juxtaposed, could contrast, or could even complement each other in some way. The machine and tool images do not necessarily have to transform the earth . . . it could be the other way around, or something completely different. For this exercise, think about things that are going through metamorphosis and what they begin as, how (and possibly why) they transform, and what they end up as. Make this a very physical poem, gutsy, gritty, intense, noisy.

Example

In this example, Emma uses the transformation of animals into cuts of meat (literally colliding with steel) as an extended metaphor for traffic on a Sunday morning.

Sunday Morning Traffic

Heavy, holy animals
charge through dirt streets,
wiry hair covered with sty-mud
from the young rice paddies
winding through the mountains
with smooth calligraphy curves
in golden ink.

In the morning, their long bodies are
strung up, embracing dawn
with rough ax cuts
dragged across torsos.
Hung from rusting iron hooks,
they make their way to market
to be quartered and weighed, divided and sold
for pocket change and dumpling soup.

Blunt cleavers smash through
bones, saving every piece of flesh
to be packaged in thin plastic
on worn wooden tables.
From their shrink wrap
covers, ravaged again by
cold steel, they are reborn
into stir fries then given back
to the earth once more to
nourish their kin.

—*Emma Burke*

Reclaiming Our Environment

This exercise perhaps reverses the idea of the "Manufactured Landscape" or
"Earth in Transformation" exercises. What if we were able to undo the damage we have done to the earth? What would it look like to have an unpolluted
world—and perhaps just as interestingly, what would the process of unpollut-
ing the world look like? Consider the things that contribute to the pollution
of the world—manufacturing, overpopulation, war, chemicals, noise pollution,
light pollution, etc. Even if the changed landscape was for the positive, what
would it be like if nature reclaimed its space?

The Exercise

Write a poem that explores the idea of reversing the damage humans have done
to the earth. Be specific (for example, concentrate on nuclear waste or noise pollution or war). Try to give the poem images and a context that leave the reader
grounded and that will help it avoid sounding preachy. Use descriptors, metaphors, juxtapositions, and other techniques to let the images carry an implied
rather than explicit feeling.

Example

Hey Kurt

And from the air
we take back the smoke—
vacuum the dark clouds
into our long chimneys

and swiftly disassemble the components
until it is air again.

And out of the factories pour the
dark earth treasures,
sinking back into the deep cavities
where they wait
for centuries
until a force which deserves them
uncovers their earth with wind
and begins to secrete
their mystery.

—*Lilly Lerer*

Activism

Writing and activism go hand in hand. Writing is anything but passive. It is an active voice in the fray of human struggle. Writers have always inspired those around them to stand up for a better life on this planet. Poems of activism, those that shine a light on social justice issues, call for peace, give a voice to the voiceless, or are the words of those who speak out on their own behalf, are some of the most important and powerful poems out there. It is no wonder that authoritarian regimes often jail, persecute, exile, or assassinate poets.

The Exercise

Write a poem that celebrates activism in some way—peace advocacy, environmental conservation, the struggle for freedom and human rights, etc. These could be your own efforts or the efforts of others, something historical or contemporary, something near or far. Don't let the piece become preachy (which most often happens when we forego images for exposition). So, instead, collect the images of those actions and the people involved. Invoke a tone/create a mood that exemplifies the struggle at hand. In exemplifying a struggle or shining a light on social justice issues, remember that offering or casting a vision for a solution can be powerful but is not always necessary—sometimes simply education or inspiring is called for.

Example

1967

I thought about you when
the sun plunged to your rolling green hills
when your sons ravaged barren fields,
their bodies
bored through with hunger and hatred:
savage animals, untamed beasts

so when, that night you called for me
wordless, soundless
called for me
I sent my children
all in neat little rows, dressed up with
their paper arsenals

my noble joe,
my rebel jane

I sent my children.

—*Caitlyn Le*

Poetry Triathlon

This poem encourages approaching writing as a physical act and helps to connect intangible ideas and experiences to the tangible world around us. But the process of writing is not simply one that begins inside and travels outside. The external world—the physical things and space around us, even our own physical movements and bodies—has strong influence over what then happens to us internally. The writing of this poem requires you to move, interact with your environment, and write in response. Think of Wordsworth taking brisk walks through the Lake District before writing a poem.

The Exercise
Write a poem in three sections based on the following three ideas. The sections do not need to relate, though finding a common center for the poem would certainly be a strength. For this poem, the subject can be about what you are

experiencing, but it might be best if the subject were something else and the sounds, movements, and rhythms you experience influence the images, sounds, movements, and rhythms of what you write.

1. Run wildly, and silently, with pen and paper rippling under intense velocity. Run until your heart beats madly. Quickly write the first section of the poem before your heartbeats dissipate back into something more still.

2. Find a mechanism of some sort—this could be a full machine, or it could just be something with moving (mechanical parts). Turn it, move it, feel it, hear it. Write.

3. Find some water. Interact with it in some way. Write. Don't use the word *water* or any sort of fancy euphemism for it.

After writing all three sections, take some time to shape and edit your material so that the final poem, while still consisting of three sections, finds some unity in imagery, theme, and style.

Example

Approaching Dusk

I.
Towards the edge of the earth
where I let myself fall
into the Cimmerian shade
is a fish
who floats on the periphery
and gasps for air
like I do.

II.
I scoop him up,
cradling his bloated stomach
and running my finger down his scales
with all smoothness
as if he were the volume dial
turned down
so low
only I could enjoy it.

III.
But when I try to close my hand into a fist
he pours out the side,
spilling through my fingers
and I smile,
having felt
the drape of his thirst
wash over me.

—*An Rhiel Wang*

Dropping a Mouse into a Poem

Billy Collins asks us in "Introduction to Poetry" to reconsider how we approach a poem, to read and imagine it in a natural way. He advises his audience, among other things, to put a mouse into a poem, suggesting that doing so would change our view of the poem's natural space. What if we reenvisioned our own poems in such a light? Would they, as we viewed them through a lens other than the critical voice, need to be revised or read in special ways? What if we radically, even arbitrarily, transformed our work to allow it to shift into new contexts, address different subjects, and include uninvited imagery?

Recommended Poem

Collins, Billy. "Introduction to Poetry." *Poetry 180: A Turning Back to Poetry*. Random House, 2003. Collins's poem is also available at the Poetry 180 website: www.loc .gov/poetry/180/001.html

The Exercise

Take any poem you have written previously and drop a mouse into it. Let a mouse enter the life and space of the poem and maybe even try to get back out. Rewrite that poem with the mouse present in the new version. Is he part of the setting? Does he become a character? Does he break the wall between author and characters? Does he turn the poem philosophically upon its head, engendering a wholly new perspective on something? Does he fit seamlessly? Is he a tiny blip in the corner? Does he offer a contrasting or a parallel image to something already there?

Example

In the example below, although the "mouse" version is mostly similar to its original, the addition of that image, especially as a first line, adds important characterization to the poem as well as develops the tone even more. The changed title and other added imagery in line 2 support this direction for the tone to make the poem increasingly fragile and vulnerable. You can decide whether you think of the mouse as literal or a metaphor.

Original poem:

Swiftly Striking Lightning Bugs

Too light now from
Losing all her
Remembrances,
She spins wildly
Into the sky
Falling away
From gauzy lime dreams

"Mouse" version:

Punched Tin Constellations

Daughter of a mouse,
she was born hiding
in a wooden womb, but
too light now from
losing all her
remembrances,
she spins wildly
into the sky
falling away
from gauzy lime dreams.

—*Emma Burke*

Making Beasts: The Mythology of Creatures

The creatures of our childhood, many of which we create ourselves, populate an area that helped us traverse our fears. I still remember well the lion-like beast that sat on my bed. Terrified as I was when I dreamed it (half-awake), I recall that it seemed to call me not to be eaten, but to follow courageously. Sometimes we fashion beasts—or masks—or the accessories of a myth (most commonly a weapon such as a sword)—from twigs and branches, leaves, stones, or even draw them in dirt or with chalk. Our making them allows us to interact with them in a more powerful way, a way in which we can be the myth-maker instead of being made by the beast.

Recommended Poem

Orr, Gregory. "Making Beasts." *The Caged Owl: New and Selected Poems.* Copper Canyon Press, 2002.

The Exercise

Write a poem about a beast you created. Maybe you drew it as a child; maybe you just imagined it or dreamed of it. Maybe the beast was an imaginary friend of sorts, or perhaps it haunted or stalked you. Maybe the beast was just a product of the objects around you inspiring some sort of two- or three-dimensional collage or other visual representation (think of arranging stones into figure-like shapes or turning a sock into a monster-like puppet). Try to focus on the unique nature of what you created, not relying on the "monster in the closet" trope, but defining the specific features that played with your psyche.

Example

In this example, the death of Graceanne's dog triggers a memory of a "human" beast that feeds off of her own imagined monster: a "forty-seven" eyed beast. Graceanne does a fine job of weaving her own beast into the psychological impact of other events and images in her life and mind.

Beasts

My dog saw God yesterday.
Her ashes, half a shoebox full,
felt warmer than the space
heater, webbed and
forgotten on my back porch.
They soothed my feathered tongue.
They tasted frothy
as fermented sea foam,
sour tree sap,
and that frozen boy

who knew my mouth better
than anyone. He
murdered three men
on a Sunday afternoon.
My needled bones lusted
for a forty-seven
eyed beast, broken
by stares and branches.
He savored that
blood pool memory
more than basement stored
jars of rotted flesh.

—*Graceanne Howard*

Library Poem

What better inspiration is there for writing than books themselves? Writers must read—not only to grow in their technical prowess, but also, and most important, to keep feeding their inner selves. This exercise encourages you to turn to your personal library for inspiration, as Albert Goldbarth does in his poem "Library," which inspired this exercise. In his poem, Goldbarth celebrates some books, regrets others, details how some changed him, or simply recalls a powerful image or idea from yet others.

Recommended Poem

Goldbarth, Albert. "Library." *Saving Lives.* Ohio University Press, 2001. "Library" is also available at Poetry Daily: http://poems.com/special_features/library.htm

The Exercises

1. Write an ode to your personal library. To cover many books, let each just occupy a line or two. Vary your observations in terms of tone, details, and the kind of influence or impact (or lack thereof) that the book may have had on you.

2. Choose one of the books in your library and explore it deeply in its own poem.

Example

Book

This book gave me magic.
This book should be read in Spanish but I couldn't do it.
This book laughs at sheep, Ireland, and murder by spade.
This book came in a large package I mistook for something I wanted.
I've kept this book open on its stomach for three years.
This book has the longest title I've ever seen and is about me, except it's not.
This book showed me a blood stain shaped like Japan and I will never remember what else.
This is the book I bought for the bloated red hand on the cover in the middle of an airport, needing only light entertainment; I fell deeply and painfully in love then gave it to my mother on the plane ride back, making her sob in front of all those strangers.
I never read this book, but I know about the purple birds anyway.
This book trapped me underwater with Helen in the freezing pond and ended before I realized I was never there, but cried anyway.
This book takes place in a circus and in Heaven.
In chapter 92 of this book, the lost boy finds a molar in what he thought was a fruit: reading it made my oatmeal look like melted, bubbling skin.
This book is the worst.
This book is a burnt hate song.
This book was important only once I found the dictionary as a sidekick.
This book has too many words for its story; the ship filled with letters capsized and spilled its waste into the murky, torpid pages.
This book is a bird, its pages, beating wings.
This book taught me I'm an idiot.
I read the last four pages of this book in the store and should have left it at that.
This book teases you with whispers, then screams for twenty pages.
This is only a song but I wish the author had kept singing and let his words fill up pages and pages.
This book crossed the border into Mexico and fit so well with the rainy season I left it there.
This book leapt down my throat and filled my stomach.
This book built a staircase up to Paris.
This book killed a magician.

—*Tory Tarpley*

Math Poem

While mathematics and poetry could not seem further apart in today's academy, they actually have a long, rich, intertwined history. Mathematics has appeared as a part of poetry as far back as poetry goes. In Sarah Glaz's article "Poetry Inspired by Mathematics: A Brief Journey through History," she describes the use of mathematics within poetry in Sumerian tablets dedicated to the moon god, Nanna, around 1800 BCE. Even Archimedes posed a mathematical challenge in verse form in his poetic word problem, "The Cattle Problem." Pure numbers can inspire poetry, and the terms and concepts of mathematics can touch a deep philosophical nerve. One can easily see this use of math in the context of thought—and even emotion—in Amy Quan Barry's poem "If $dy/dx = (4x^3 + x^2\text{-}12)/\surd(2x^2\text{-}9)$, Then."

Recommended Poems

Barry, Quan. "If $dy/dx = (4x^3 + x^2\text{-}12)/\surd(2x^2\text{-}9)$, Then." *Asylum*. University of Pittsburgh Press, 2001.

Dove, Rita. "Geometry." *Collected Poems: 1974–2004*. W.W. Norton and Company, 2016.

Neruda, Pablo. "Ode to Numbers." *All the Odes*. Farrar, Straus, and Giroux, 2017.

Szymborska, Wislawa. "Pi." *Poems New and Collected*. Harcourt Books, 2000.

Recommended Article

Glaz, Sarah. "Poetry Inspired by Mathematics: A Brief Journey through History." *Journal of Mathematics and the Arts,* vol. 5, no. 4, 2011, pp. 171–83. In addition to discussing mathematics in poetry, Glaz includes several great math poems, including Samuel Taylor Coleridge's "A Mathematical Problem" and William Bronk's "Boolean Algebra: $X^2 = X$."

The Exercise

Write a poem using a mathematical concept or term as inspiration. There are thousands to choose from: multiplication, division, addition, subtraction, remainder, the quadratic equation, algorithms, pi, angles, hypotenuse, asymptote, metrics, infinity, negative numbers, imaginary numbers, graphs, algebraic equations, derivatives, square roots, percentages, circumference, fractions, and so on. One option may be to style your poem like a word problem. Still another style may simply be in the standard lyrical mode using mathematical terms or logic to address a philosophical or emotional problem . . . or vice versa . . . applying emotion or philosophy to a mathematical equation.

Example

Allegory of The Cave

If there are 8
and 2 leave,
get up quietly and push in
their chairs,
and then another disappears,
vanishing with a crack into thin air,
then 8 become 5.
And if those 5 produce 2 each,
then there are 15 total,
and if each of their legs detach
from their bodies
and become 2 more,
then suddenly there are 30;
a joyous roomful.
And if the hands
of those 30 unfasten gently
from the end of their arms
and hover, flapping around
like in a surrealist painting,
and each finger grows into another,
then there has been a great growth.
And if those 150 are standing
in the cold,
and each hair on their
bodies releases from
their skin
and flies out of the cave,
until the air is thick and spinning with hair,
then of course there are too many hairs to count.
And if all of those hairs turn into others,
there are whole horizons of them.
And the thing to be learned from all of this, I guess,
is simply to look over your multiplication tables again
from time to time
lest they become restless
and multiply themselves.

—*Lilly Lerer*

Wondering: Philosophy, Theology, and Psychology in Poetry

Out of all the disciplines, philosophy, theology, and psychology play the largest role in the world of poetry. Poetry, using imagery, manifests our inner lives—our beliefs, our questions, our emotions, our fears, our joys. Sometimes in writing a poem, those thoughts and feelings come first, then the imagery (or vice versa), and then we see the philosophy, theology, or psychology inherent in the poem once it is completed. But it could also be helpful to begin with a philosophical or theological question or belief or a psychological concept and have the poem's imagery spring from that genesis.

The Exercise

Begin by selecting a philosophical or theological question or belief or a psychological concept and then, as you write the poem, explore what imagery would make your choice tangible for the audience. Specific imagery, consideration of audience, defining a specific voice and tone, and deciding on a type of poem (lyric or narrative, for example) is extremely important in this exercise so that the writing does not devolve into vagueness or internal monologue.

You may select anything related to these disciplines, but here are some possible topics or questions to consider:

- Philosophy: the philosopher Søren Kierkegaard wrote a series of parables based on the following questions. You could choose one to write your poem on:
  - What happens to those who try to warn the present age?
  - What is left for the philosopher to do when a society is preparing for war?
  - What is the relation of eternity and the moment?
  - Of all wishes, which is the best?
- Theology: in addition to the standard questions of theology, such as whether or not God exists, consider these questions, which often have theological implications:
  - Why does something rather than nothing exist?
  - How did the world come into being?
  - Why is there suffering in the world?
- Psychology: in addition to the standard questions one might ask in regard to psychology (or psychiatry, for that matter—"Am I crazy?" is

always a fun question!), consider writing about some terms and concepts from psychology: bias, grief, guilt, anxiety, narcissism, alter egos, self-confidence, consciousness, gratitude, zero-sum thinking, emotional intelligence, identity crisis—or any of the thousands more!

Example

In this example, also an imitation of Juan Ramón Jiménez, Shaye's speaker wonders about her place in and concept of the world, a thought framed quite nicely by the image-centered question: "So why is it they tell me the earth is round?"

Earth
after Juan Ramón Jiménez

I have a feeling that I am lost in the wilderness,
Perhaps tangled in the sea or dangled off a cliff.
On edge, flailing like a broken-winged bird.

So why is it they tell me the earth is round?
Or do only paintbrush-handed men
Find a seat on the edge of the world?

Maybe seeing is found under boulders.
Perhaps it is a well-cut ruby or topaz,
One with many polished perspectives.

—Shaye Martin

Abstract Portrait Poem

Writers have long been inspired by the visual arts, and vice versa. Brueghel's *Landscape with the Fall of Icarus* inspired important poems from both W. H. Auden and William Carlos Williams. In the twentieth century, as art began to involve more abstract forms, poetry seemed then to turn to a trend of finding inspiration in the artists rather than in the art itself. Jackson Pollock and Robert Motherwell stand as two artists that inspired many poems, but just as much for their lives, their artistic presence, or their politics as for a specific piece. But what if poets made a more conscious effort to write based on an interpretation of an abstract visual? How would one translate such lines and shapes into words? Would the resulting poem necessarily have to be abstract as well? This exercise provides a door into such an exploration.

The Exercise

Have someone draw an abstract portrait of how they are feeling. Remember that abstract art uses lines, shapes, colors, and forms to express something visual that is not reflective of the visuals of our reality. Don't discuss with the person any details of what went into their drawing or what it means. Alternatively, you could use a work of art by a famous abstract artist: Wassily Kandinsky, Sonia Delaunay, Joan Miró, Jackson Pollock, Robert Motherwell, or Mark Rothko to name just a few. To help you get a sense of the piece and how you might interpret it, look at the lines, the shapes, the colors, the forms, the busyness or sparseness, the movement (is it slow, sweeping, swift, smooth, or tremulous?), the boldness, the thinness, the way items interact with other items. Write a poem that captures these ideas and feelings in its imagery and in its own movement and even its sound.

You can also draw your own abstract portrait and give it to someone for them to write a poem. This would be another good exercise for a creative writing class or workshop.

Example

In this example, Mandy re-creates the tangled, kinetic nature of the portrait she received.

Eyes' Heat

Leg upon leg
we knotted our knees together
crevicing into each other's corners.
Your hands rub against the slow turns
that skin makes against stomach.

Open your eyes—
Reel your kited thoughts back in.

—*Mandy Cline*

The Seriousness of Cartoons

Cartoons hold a strange and powerful place in our world, a genre unto themselves. As children, we are thrilled by them, entertained, opened to a world of humor, whimsy, danger, and imagination. As adults, they can reignite our imagination, and we find within them sometimes difficult truths about our world. They are a place ripe for paradox.

In his poem "Commercial Break: Road-Runner, Uneasy," Tim Seibles explores the absurdity of Road-Runner and Coyote's relationship. As the speaker of the poem, Road-Runner remarks on the bizarre nature of roles, breaks down the wall between cartoon and reality, and speaks for us as well as for himself.

Whereas Seibles uses cartoons to look at roles and relationships, in "Cartoon Physics, Part I," Nick Flynn looks at the laws of the natural world versus the laws of imagination. What a complex view of the world, that recognizes the dangers that surround us but can also laugh at them and try to subdue them with the power of the imagination.

Recommended Poems

Flynn, Nick. "Cartoon Physics, Part I." *Some Ether*. Graywolf Press, 2000. Flynn's poem is also available at Poetry 180: www.loc.gov/poetry/180/038.html

Seibles, Tim. "Commercial Break: Road-Runner, Uneasy." *Hammerlock: Poems*, Cleveland State University Poetry Center, 1999.

The Exercise

Write a poem that uses the imagery of cartoons to communicate a truth about human nature, relationships, our world, our fears, dangers, the tragedy or triumph of life, and so on. The imagery might come from a specific cartoon, or it might be generic cartoon imagery.

Example

Three Years After Tom and Jerry's Contract Ran Out

Dry ribs rattling in a grocery bag, the cat
slept by the street.
The black and tailed manna
took a stroll, on a whim.
Bony fingers tickled a scythe
as the breeze awoke.

—*Tory Tarpley*

Advertisements

Inspiration, emotions, memories, art, relationships—our world surrounds us with things that impact our inner lives on a daily, if not moment by moment, basis. Some of these things impact us positively, some negatively, some dramatically, some subtly. Some of these things we let impact us, others force themselves upon us, and some of the influence is subconscious. Whether we like it or not, especially in the growing material nature of a capitalist society that has seen unparalleled technological progress in the past one hundred years, advertisements play a large role in the stream of images and ideas that enter our psyche. Advertisements perhaps don't deserve to be categorized as art in and of themselves, especially because of their purpose, but they work with visual, auditory, and linguistic elements to consciously or subconsciously change us, just as art does.

The Exercise

Write a poem that explores an advertisement that moved you (for good or bad), annoyed you, confused you, tempted you, distracted you, angered you, or made you laugh, cry, or sigh. Think about the many forms of advertisements: billboards, commercials, infomercials, lawn signs, jingles, internet pop-ups, sales calls, product placement, junk mail, fliers, and classified ads.

Example

Closed Doors

I should've pretended like I didn't see her
Crying, on the couch, messily wiping off tears
But as that life insurance commercial came on,
I couldn't help it—if I thought it, she did too.
All these old people on the screen, smiling, saying,

"When my husband died, I was ready for a life
Of independence." Another happily said,
"When I'm gone, I know my family will be ready."

All of them, speaking as if

Death was an opportunity.

What am I not seeing?

—*Isabella So*

Questioning

Questions work in intricate ways in poetry. I often see students try to use rhetorical questions or ask themselves questions in the midst of a piece, yet those so often fall flat. What constitutes a good question? Some work in their simplicity; some work in their complexity. Some are universal; some are incredibly specific. Some are meant to be answered; others are not. Some may seem to hold a unique, singular place in a poem, as if, childlike, a question spontaneously appeared, creating both fragmentation and mystery. Most questions in poetry, though, fit within the surrounding context and offer a way for the poem to engage the reader (more so than a way for the writer to reflect).

Pablo Neruda has an entire book of poems composed solely of questions. His work may be the pinnacle in questioning. I've also always loved the different questions James Wright asks in his poem "Hook." In particular, Wright questions the audience as to whether they have felt a particular experience and object (a man's prosthetic hook), and while in the context of this poem our answer might at first be "no," upon further consideration of the poem, of what Wright is saying in a universal sense, and of what we might have experienced in parallel, the answer could be "yes." Though it may not have been a man's prosthetic hook we felt, we may well have had this surreal and vulnerable moment in some other way. Wright asks the question in just the right way so that we at once understand the bizarre nature of his experience but also feel drawn into it in understanding.

Recommended Poem

Wright, James. "Hook." *Above the River: The Complete Poems.* Farrar, Straus, and Giroux, 1992.

Recommended Book

Neruda, Pablo. *The Book of Questions.* Copper Canyon Press, 2001.

The Exercise

Write a poem that uses questions in an interesting, unexpected way, using as a model either Neruda (composing a poem completely of questions) or Wright (asking a question that both lays out a specific, individual experience and a universal invitation to the reader to find a parallel moment). You might also consider questioning a character, an object, a metaphor, even a word or image in the poem directly.

Example

Cancer

The golden dusk
painted itself onto canvas behind you
and I could almost feel

the sunflower whispers against the
rough collar of your bathrobe.

You stroked my hair
and told me you loved me
in the resonant voice of a Stradivari cello
a voice rich with years of
cigar smoke
and Vietnam.

Who is the shadow hiding
in the corner of the canvas?
Do you know its name?

No, but it's waiting for me.

—*Antonia Buban*

Modern Frame for a Classic Theme

Love, loss, relationships, death, fear, spirituality—so much of what we write about has been addressed by artists throughout the ages. How should we present such material? Is there anything new to say about family, good, evil, nature, or heroism? I have too often seen writers revert to archaic imagery and language when exploring a "classic" theme. This exercise encourages a contemporary perspective, one that involves a fresh take on a classic theme.

The Exercise
Imagine a relationship and what "theme" might define that relationship: love, family, fear, evil, spirituality, heroism, etc. Imagine an interaction that represents that relationship: a series of gestures, a conversation, letters exchanged, a trail of neglect or ignoring. Frame those things within modern (twenty-first-century) life—technology, capitalism, paranoia, busyness, advertising. The following example uses several of these themes in a subtle way.

Example
In this example, Mandy explores the classic theme of a relationship growing distant, using the modern imagery of static and pixilation as a metaphor to re-create the dissolution.

Scene

I couldn't remember any of the conversations we had today.
They were static-y fragments of a dream.
Your face,
pixeled out along with your hair
and skin and eyes.
That's not how the
script goes.

—*Mandy Cline*

Anti-ing: Using Prefixes and Suffixes

Conscious of it or not, we often find our inspiration for or the genesis of a poem in things that are whole (a whole object, a whole word or sentence, etc.). Dutch bank ING once had a brilliant advertising campaign: they put their company name on the back of a bus bench, but placed it to the right side instead of centered. Thus, when someone sat in the center of the bench or to the left, the person plus the visible *ing* produced a living narrative. Whatever that person was doing (reading, talking, even just sitting) made the *ing* come to life. I felt moved as I reflected on the power of that suffix. This exercise plays with that idea, extending it to other suffixes as well as prefixes.

The Exercises

1. *Anti-*: Some opposites are easy to find . . . black and white, war and peace, narrow and wide. But other objects or ideas might have more obscure opposites. What is the opposite of a nickel or a book? I propose that the opposite wouldn't just be something similar (such as a dime or a piece of paper as opposites of the nickel or book), but it would be something that reverses qualities of that object so that if it were real and tangible, it could only be used in an opposite way, or in a context different from its normal one. Think of something that does not clearly have an opposite and find for it an appropriate opposite. Then write a poem about how that opposite would operate, how it would be used, and what kind of world or context it would be used in. As always, your object/opposite pair might be concrete and tangible, or they might be used as metaphor.

2.   *-ing*: Write a poem that explores states of action and their relationship to states of being. Think about how adding the suffix *ing* brings actions and states of being to life (particularly as adding this suffix usually creates a present participle or gerund, parts of speech that embody action). Avoid the temptation to simply list *-ing* words, as it may seem that they carry enough active weight. Rather, you must build images around those words that place them in context and create for them a purposeful tone.

3.   Write a poem inspired by any other prefix or suffix: *un-, multi-, over-, super-, -ish, -less, -able,* and so on.

Example

In this example, An Rhiel executes the *-ing* exercise perfectly, relating the actions (climbing, screaming, and treading) to her states of being ("I am the hilltop," "I am the song," and "I am the water," respectively).

> **-ing**
>
> I am the hilltop you are climbing
> with pink-eyed puppets in your fists.
>
> I am the song you are screaming
> when you fall into the foxhole.
>
> I am the water you are treading
> as you drown.
>
> —*An Rhiel Wang*

Poetic Résumé

Unlike a résumé, a poem values the subjective, the sublime, and the ethereal over the objective, concrete, quantifiable experience. Not only is a résumé full of material, corporeal happenings, its aims are material as well. But what if our *poetic* résumé helped us apply for something transcendent? What if our job résumés sounded more like poems?

Recommended Poem

Szymborska, Wislawa. "Writing a Résumé." *View with a Grain of Sand: Selected Poems.* Harcourt Brace, 1995.

The Exercise

Write a "poetic résumé." That is, write a poem that addresses who you are, what you've accomplished, what you might want to project about your personality, your background, your dreams, your intended future. Play with the imagery, perhaps satirizing the generic images that might tend to arise in a résumé, but also offering some surprises—personal or descriptive details where details might not normally be, or information you might not normally include but that certainly speaks to who you are. You might consider writing it in résumé format, or simply presenting it as a lyric or narrative poem, but one that addresses the identity- and accomplishment-establishing purposes of a résumé.

Example

In this example, rather than use the form of a résumé, Alex chooses to write a lyric poem, using intense imagery to build a record of all that she is, has achieved, and has experienced in that internal/poetic sense. Alex also uses several effective sound techniques in this poem.

Turn Around

I am grass floating up to your windowsill
I am a cloud in a shallow room
I am burning wind
I am your music
I am my music
I am crawling
I am,
I am.

Inside my ribs, you won't find a smoke signal . . .
You will find a sticky tornado
It will cause you to be lost
Trust me, you will not arrive at a brick road

—*Alex Edwards*

Part of Me

Some things that are part of us make sense: our families; a tragic event; a physical attribute such as a birthmark or scar; a childhood home or creek or tree house. But there are also things that shape and constitute who we are that are more difficult to explain: a trinket that we lost, such as a certain toy airplane; an encounter with an acquaintance; a meaningless gesture that has become a habit—things that on the surface seem inconsequential, but because of something in their nature or because of their context, they establish a defining presence in our psyche. Much like the "Poetic Résumé" exercise, this exercise is about identity, though here you will explore one specific part of your identity in detail.

The Exercise

Choose an object, action, or encounter that might seem inconsequential but that you would actually say is a "part of you." Use detailed imagery to place what you have chosen in a specific context, whether that context is real (such as the setting for the encounter) or an imagined/metaphorical one.

Example

Observations, 10/13/09

This quilt is a part of me
like the cries of the crickets outside
and the paper about capitalism
that my brother asks me to edit
and the way a thick fog
has permeated the neighborhood
tonight, diffracting
thin rainbow circles
around the porch lights.

And "a part of me"
means this:
I cannot know profound joy
greater than
this handful of world
silently converting
into my own inwardness.

—*Lilly Lerer*

I Am Not

This exercise is the exact opposite of the "Part of Me" and "Poetic Résumé" exercises. Instead of defining ourselves by what we are, what we have experienced or achieved, or what has influenced us, what if we defined ourselves by what we are not?

The Exercise

Start by creating a list of fifteen to twenty things that you are *not*. Use very specific imagery. Think metaphorically. Think about simple, everyday images just as much as you would large-scale images that too easily invoke identity. From that list, use your favorite five to ten images to create a poem that boldly proclaims what you are *not*. You might, at one point, state what you *are* to create a dramatic moment, but keep the focus on what you are *not*.

Example

Any Other Peanut

I am not like any other peanut forever smeared on the floor of Yankee Stadium.
I do not beat in Einstein's right brain lobe as millions of cells unanimously did.
I am not just ordinary bamboo that bends inside avant-garde banisters.

I am Alive, a smile that disassembles frowns,
not another positioned white pin on your white wall,
nor the tightly closed bud of a morning glory,
instead, a resonance of golden hornet stings that each glisten as the world revolves.

— *Alexia Garcia-Tyler*

The Bright Side

Poetry that is all dark or all light can easily attract criticism. All dark, and you run the risk of turning off the reader with a nihilistic portrait of the world. All light, and you run the risk of sounding naïve. Both extremes in imagery quite often also happen to display poor technique. A poem that mixes light and dark/positive and negative sometimes has a better chance of displaying the ebb and flow/yin and yang of life. This has its risks, too—in fact, the title of this exercise is a risk. Finding the bright side of things risks cliché and naïveté, but when presented with surprising images, the idea can reenter our consciousness in a way that restores our faith.

The Exercise

Write a small poem, between two and ten lines, that at first presents something dark, negative, unwanted, or that carries a negative connotation, but resolves itself into something light, wanted, or that carries a positive connotation.

Example

While Emily's use of the word *beautiful* in the first line may immediately rehabilitate the possible negativity of the first line, I still believe that the negative connotations of both the "cliché" and the mass-market appeal of a blockbuster are best resolved through the charming image of the new popcorn maker in the small town theater.

Our Love

A beautiful cliché that made millions in a box office
helped a small town theatre buy a popcorn maker.

—Emily Nielson

Writing about Loss

There is perhaps no greater purpose and no greater challenge in writing than to address loss—significant loss. This loss most often is the loss of a loved one. Sometimes it is the loss of innocence, sometimes of something physical such as one's sight or a limb. These are experiences so intense and bewildering that they can leave the most talented and professional writers with wordless babble.

Writing about loss well is really no different from writing about anything else—establishing your voice, considering your audience, using effective and specific imagery—but in the end, writing about loss well is perhaps even more about finding your imaginative and emotional footing even when those things seem to be spinning out of control. It is an act of courage and a supreme act of hope. Even when we feel the most despair and even when we write proclaiming despair, that we are still writing and communicating exhibits hope in a transcendent way. This exercise suggests a few techniques, more as reminders, but ultimately, to write about loss well is a personal journey that one simply must go through to learn.

The Exercise

Write about a significant loss: the loss of a loved one, a physical/bodily loss, a home lost to fire or flood, the death of a dream. It may be helpful to spend some time prewriting and making lists of specific images that represent that person or thing lost rather than the pain of the loss itself. In the end, for the sake of yourself and others, find the courage to share your piece—not only will it be a wonderful gift to others, but with the idea of audience in mind, you are more likely to write something lasting.

Example

While it would be easy to point out Alex's exemplary technique in the following poem, what I most appreciate and celebrate is her bravery and her gift to us all in sharing this.

A Letter to My Father

One day I will release your ashes onto the Alaskan glaciers
And you will form blue wings
On that day I need you to remind me why
Your stairway to heaven required you to fall fifteen stories
After I let you go, come visit me
Be the fire underneath my fingernails
Remind me what it means to fight

—*Alex Edwards*

Tragic Events

The "Writing about Loss" exercise encourages an exploration of personal loss, but sometimes loss and tragic events are played out on a national or international scale. We often need to process these events just as much as personal loss. Giving attention to such events beyond ourselves teaches us so much about empathy and social justice, and giving voice to our sorrow or outrage gives us agency to care for the world in a more active way. Doing so also lends support to those directly impacted who are telling their stories and gives voice to those impacted who are not able to tell their stories.

Whenever we do give our perspective on something we did not directly experience, we must be careful in several respects. We must not assume that we have the answers, we must not presume to know exactly how someone else might feel, and we must always, always speak out of compassion (even if our feeling and our tone is outrage)—the purpose is not to preach, but to empathize, connect, support, and advocate.

The Exercise

Write a poem about a tragic event that you are troubled by. This event may be a current event, or it may be one from history. It need not be something as large as the Holocaust, though such an event is worthy of and has generated much wonderful and important art. At times, especially with a large tragic event, it can be helpful to choose one smaller story, perhaps the story of one person, to focus on. Also consider events that have been overlooked or events that speak to you in a way that they may not speak to others. In your imagery, don't shy away from showing difficult things, but also keep purpose in mind—your goal is likely not to shock, but rather to speak truth and shed light.

Example

Subterranean Tragedy

In February of 2003, an arson attack on a South Korean subway train claimed over 140 lives and left many more injured.

The rusty stench of burnt hair, shoes, and clothes,
just pale whispers of the heat trickling into your pores,
swallowing up your charred skin.

Soot drapes itself over the walls like a netted black veil,
white marks peek out here and there,
minute scratches on the charcoal surface
as if someone had ticked off your deaths on a chalkboard
    child gone,
    mother gone,
    father gone,
the haunting scrapes of blunted nails.

The funny ways we console ourselves
with flowered shrines, paper cup candles, mourning banners.
"Let's tear this useless place down so we can build over it."
"Bastard, would you feel the same,
if your daughter had died here too?"
We now keep scavenged chunks of your hair in clear, plastic bags.

The melted glass framing the exit sign droops downwards,
forming misshapen, translucent fingers,
they had kissed the rising hell.

Sighs clamber past that dusty granite corridor.
Remember me,
    Remember me,
        Remember me,
Remember to leave me flowers by the stairs.

—*Patricia Lee*

4

Bolt and Arc: Poems That Use and Transcend Form

Introduction

The path of a lightning bolt is stunningly beautiful, but what impresses most, particularly if one is on the receiving end, is the nature and the impact of that lightning. If, midway in its path to the ground, the bolt had zigged instead of zagged, but ultimately fell in the same place, no one would be the wiser, nor would one find the power of that lightning lessened. Such is the power of the poem of form. With its pragmatic sensibilities, the Western mind has obsessively turned the poem of form into a product, a tangible thing about material outcomes. Thus, readers labor to discover that a poem is a sonnet once they scan its fourteen lines, but too rarely remembering its spiritual cry or its deep mourning. Likewise, we have taken Eastern forms, as with the haiku, and slavishly attended to the 5/7/5 rule, all the while ignoring that in English, this would result in far too many syllables versus the haiku in Japanese.

In a book of exercises designed to reawaken the writer's mind to sensibilities found at deeper levels of consciousness, I offer a section on poems of form with great caution. However, I believe that many of the forms herein, properly considered, engender exactly that kind of reawakening, one in which the writer can use a path to realign to something more natural at the subconscious level, rather than something contrived, which is a real risk with a poem of form. I include here particularly forms of Eastern and Middle Eastern origin as these forms, and these cultures, are often much more attuned to how form and order result in awakening rather than in neat packaging. Other exercises, such as "Tiny Poem" or "Two-Line Poem," are almost less about form and more about intense concentration, which brings about awareness or epiphany. And some exercises such as "Elegies and Odes to People" and "Ars Poetica" explore types of poems.

Landay

A landay is a short, two-line poem. Persian in origin, it literally means "the short one." The first line consists of nine syllables, and the second consists of thirteen. A form of poetry primarily found in Afghanistan, a landay is not necessarily about the speaker, but involves the speaker's participation in some way (part of a relationship).

A landay, unlike other Persian forms, does not exalt mystical love, nor engage in wordplay or other high literary techniques. It is simple and deals with common, earthly concerns: love, suffering, war, nature, beauty, death. The imagery in a landay is often of common things, but the voices therein are bold. Such brief songs, landays often do not have titles.

In addition to reading the following student examples, I highly recommend reading authentic examples from Afghanistan. The incredible anthology *Songs of Love and War: Afghan Women's Poetry*, edited by the late Sayd Bahodine Majrouh, collects landays from anonymous Pashtun women. The article recommended below also collects numerous landays and provides a thorough background for and analysis of the landay form.

Recommended Article

Griswold, Eliza, and Seamus Murphy. "Landays." The Poetry Foundation. www.poetry foundation.org/media/landays.html

Recommended Book

Majrouh, Sayd Bahodine, editor. *Songs of Love and War: Afghan Women's Poetry*. Translated by Marjolijn de Jager. Other Press, 2010.

The Exercise

Write a landay that explores a specific moment within some great experience of love, suffering, war, nature, beauty, or death. When first composing, keep the syllable requirement, nine syllables for the first line and thirteen syllables for the second line, in the back of your mind. First concentrate on creating two or three images that are simple, but that resonate; images that can create incredible tension or release when placed together. Only when you have images that make you want to weep, shout, or roar should you then craft each chosen word and syllable to fit the syllabic goal. Ultimately, what is most important is the spirit and the voice of the landay, although musicality is a concern not to be overlooked as well. Landays usually do not have a title, though you may use one if it helps you to establish a theme.

Examples

I wish that, just once, the sweet knockings
Were your tender pebbles, not the dismayed cicadas.

—*Allie Heck*

Your scent twines between my fingertips,
But you departed in a balloon from my locked doors.

—*Katherine Lin*

Tell me what you wrote in the letter,
The one that was lost fifty years ago in the sea.

—*Katherine Lin*

Ghazal

Dating back to as early as the twelfth century, the ghazal is one of the most beautiful and challenging forms of poetry, challenging in the way that it requires both gut-wrenching emotional honesty and searing philosophical thought. In translation, the ghazal seems as if it has few technical requirements beyond that it is written in couplets, but the form in its original language (which could be Urdu, Arabic, Pashtu, or any other language from nearby regions) is indeed quite complicated, involving rules based on rhythm, rhyme, refrains, and sequence. This exercise will focus on the character of a ghazal rather than technical specifications.

In essence, a ghazal is a song of lament and love (earthly and divine) that asks agonizing philosophical questions, observes profound truths, and is both highly emotional and very much spiritual. In a ghazal, one is sometimes unsure if the author is writing about a lover or a god. Some of the original languages that ghazals were written in supported this effort, with the word for lover/god being interchangeable.

A ghazal is written in loosely related couplets (usually at least five). The loose association between couplets allows for an otherworldliness, one that is resonant even in the twenty-first century. Because the couplets are only loosely related around the theme (which is sometimes stated or suggested in the title, but sometimes only inferred by the entire poem), there can seem to be an abrupt jump from couplet to couplet. This happens occasionally, with other couplets seeming to fit together more naturally. Many couplets can work almost epigrammatically or aphoristically.

As with the "Landay" exercise, you will definitely want to read some ghazals beyond the student example. Ghalib is most highly recommended.

Recommended Books

Ghalib, Mirza Asadullah Khan. *The Lightning Should Have Fallen on Ghalib*. Translated by Robert Bly and Sunil Dutta. Ecco Press, 1999. Two poems by Ghalib can be found at Poetry Foundation: www.poetryfoundation.org/poems-and-poets/poets/detail/mirza-asadullah-khan-ghalib#about

Lorca, Federico García. *The Tamarit Poems*. Translated by Michael Smith. Dedalus Press, 2002. Lorca includes twelve ghazals in this collection, though some of them differ quite a bit in style and content from traditional ghazals.

Rumi. *The Book of Rumi: Ruba'is, Ghazals, Masnavis, a Qasida & Tarikh-bands*. Translated by Paul Smith. New Humanity Books, 2014.

The Exercise

Thinking of a lament, a love, an agonizing question, or a profound truth that resonates on both earthly and divine planes, write a ghazal. Keep some of these goals and possibilities in mind:

- The form should present a series of loosely related couplets that center on the spiritual/philosophical/metaphysical/emotional question or state of being.

- Strike a grand, philosophical/spiritual/melodramatic tone, while still using specific images; maybe even consider using questions (look at the specificity of Ghalib's questions for a good model).

- Write as though the poem could be addressed to a god, a lover, or some other presence that has immense psychological, spiritual, or emotional power. That presence could even be some specific aspect of self.

Example

Our Nature

Oh brown fox,
The world is glutted with birthmarks shaped like your eyes

Your hair is iridescence and untouched
Like a newborn child

Why must all innocence be plunged out of the Earth with a
    volcanic burst?
Why must all beauty be withheld by the rain?

Oh brown fox,
Speak to me with your feet

Tap the floorboard, scratch the wallpaper,
Smear the dirt on my heart

I'm ready,
Are you?

—*Alex Edwards*

Haiku

Haiku are without a doubt one of the most popular forms of poetry. They are at once accessible and exciting, capturing brief moments of experience. A sixteenth-century form of Japanese lyric poetry, haiku are traditionally written with seventeen syllables over the course of three lines—five syllables, seven, and then five again. But these syllable rules apply primarily to Japanese. Due to the differences between Japanese and English in terms of how words and syllables work, seventeen syllables in English say much more than in Japanese, thus making a seventeen-syllable English-language haiku much wordier and less difficult to write. Instead of sticking religiously to the syllable rule, many modern English-language haiku writers opt to work for the spirit of the haiku: that a brief moment or an image or two might be communicated as part of a powerful experience in as few words as possible. Many serious modern haiku writers might then compose lines of three syllables / five syllables / three syllables . . . or 4/5/4 . . . or very short/short/very short. Translators of Japanese haiku often operate by these ideas as well.

These features often guide the technique and content of haiku:

- The imagery often comes from nature. To say that it is a "nature" poem may be misleading, however. Like the Romantics, haiku writers are interested in the complications of nature—observing and feeling the impact of a dynamic world—not merely recording information scientifically.

- It might allude to religious beliefs, historical events, or people.

- It should create an emotional response in the reader.

- According to poet and professor Jack Myers: "[I]t must penetrate to the heart of its theme in a sudden epiphany" (known in Buddhism as satori).
- Haiku often involve juxtaposition in order both to preserve the concision of the poem and to produce content that resonates in immediacy.

Recommended Book

Bashō. *On Love and Barley: Haiku of Bashō*. Translated by Lucien Stryk. Penguin Classics, 1986.

The Exercise

Write a haiku. Rather than follow the 5/7/5 rule for the syllable count of the three lines, aim for lines that are very short/short/very short. Beyond aiming to be succinct, consider the elements of a haiku mentioned above. Most haiku do not have titles, though adding a title could give the poem another level of meaning.

Examples

School

This zero
is my way
of surviving.

—*Lilly Lerer*

Bosphorus Haiku

I am sick of girls!
Find me with the jellyfish,
they are soft and clean.

—*Lilly Lerer*

Istanbul Haiku

It's bright in Taxim.
The sidewalks are floating by . . .
no one seems to care!

—*Lilly Lerer*

Elegies and Odes to People

Beyond writing to understand our own experiences, one of the great aims of poetry can be writing to honor or address another person. This type of poetry turns inner feelings outward. An elegy, a poem that honors someone who has passed, takes both love and grief and turns them outward to share with the world. With a poem addressed to someone living, the poem might work as a celebration, like an ode, or it might be a condemnation or a call to action—the tone might take a very different tack based on your feelings about the person. The "person" addressed could also be a group of people, as with Charles Simic's poem "A Letter." Elegies and odes may or may not use apostrophe, but for young writers, it can be helpful, especially when writing about something deeply personal, to imagine a specific audience.

Recommended Poems

Simic, Charles. "The Hearse" and "A Letter." *The Voice at 3:00 A.M.: Selected Late & New Poems*. Harvest Books, 2006.

Wright, Franz. "For Donald Justice." *God's Silence*. Knopf, 2008.

Recommended Books

Gilbert, Sandra M., editor. *Inventions of Farewell: A Book of Elegies*. W.W. Norton & Company, 2001.

Neruda, Pablo. *One Hundred Love Sonnets*. Translated by Stephen Tapscott. University of Texas Press, 2014. A love poem can, in some cases, read like an ode. Neruda is particularly good at this, as his poems often celebrate an aspect of his love's features, such as her hair.

The Exercise

Write an ode about or an elegy for a person. For the purposes of this exercise, consider addressing the person directly. Letting that person become the audience can heighten the intensity of the voice with which you write. Whether they are the audience or not, be careful to avoid "insider" references (inside jokes, images, etc.).

Example

For My Dad

Tonight the sky
Freed its crystal stars
Onto us
Night has never felt this good

Quickly it
Turns into day like
Your winter hair
Turned into eternal dust

In the morning
The Earth's flowers bellowed
And asked me where you were
I responded with
"He is the veins in my body
And the water in yours"

You decided to die
I decided to live

— *Alex Edwards*

Ars Poetica

"Ars Poetica," which translates as "The Art of Poetry," is a poem written by Roman poet Horace around 19 BCE. The poem is about poetry itself and offers advice to poets about reading, writing, and sharing their work. Many other poets have written poems that are about poetry, that consist of advice to poets, or that contain an "artist's statement," wherein the poet explains why and how they write. Archibald MacLeish writes one, also called "Ars Poetica," though not all such poems use this title. Writing your own "Ars Poetica" can help make what you believe about writing and how you work as a writer conscious, which, in turn, makes those things more accessible and potent when you turn to write.

Recommended Poems

Horace. "Ars Poetica." *Horace: Satires, Epistles, and Ars Poetica*. Harvard University Press, 1929.

MacLeish, Archibald. "Ars Poetica." *Collected Poems 1917–1982*. Houghton Mifflin, 1985. MacLeish's "Ars Poetica" is also available at the Poetry Foundation: www.poetry foundation.org/poetrymagazine/poems/detail/17168

The Exercise

Write an "Ars Poetica," a statement about what you believe poetry is, what a poet is, why you write, or how you or others should write. Think of it as an artist's statement, filling it with specific imagery to re-create your world of writing. Some possibilities for those images include images of the physical presence of poems on a page, images of books (as in a library or on a desk), images of reading or writing rituals, images making the inner/intangible thought-life of a writer tangible, metaphors that communicate the spiritual power of words, and so on. You may decide to title your poem "Ars Poetica" or provide a new title that ties directly to your philosophy of writing.

Example
In this example, Caroline advises to write with heart, organically, even if imperfect, so as not to produce something so sterile that it would "cage . . . the soul."

Unfettered Melody

Scribble me a sonnet
perhaps in a Crayola spectrum of mind.
And remember not to draft
or cut or peel or sculpt too virtuosically
lest you cage the organic soul
sleeping in downy comforters
through balloon and lemon evenings.

—*Caroline Robb*

Poems to the People: Working with Sections

Many of the exercises in this book focus on the inspirational foundations of poetry—imagery and idea, primarily—but technique and form certainly go a long way in making those paths more navigable. The parts of a poem are well worth study, particularly line breaks, stanzas, and sections. This exercise focuses on sections.

Sections in a poem go much further than line breaks or stanzas in allowing a writer to create a demarcation. Those different sections may allow for changes in context, voice, tone, style, perspective, and any other shifts in authorial intent. The topic of this exercise, writing poems to various people about a subject, could certainly be altered, although writing poems addressed directly to people is a great way to learn more about voice, tone, and audience in a poem.

The Exercise
Write a poem addressing three to five people about a subject, with each address constituting one section of the poem. Are these people you have observed from

afar? Are these people you would or would not share something with? Are they unaware of something? There could be any number of reasons to address them. As you address each, build in specific imagery that carries a tone reflecting your feeling about the person, but for this poem, also don't be afraid, in a moment of heightened emotion, to state a feeling clearly and explicitly, but aimed at that person, as if in monologue.

Example

Poems to the People with Whom I Would Share a Slice of Tangerine

I.
My hand
outstretched.
Your hand
shoved into
empty pockets
or wrapped,
suffocating chess pieces
like a robe of thick wool.
You wouldn't dare
take this from me.
You wouldn't
dare.

II.
To you
who bit my cheek
and tongue,
I would give the piece
with the seed.
Oh, how I hope
that you
are left
in a public place
with a tangerine seed
in your mouth
and no napkin
or trashcan
in which to put it.

III.
Honored?
Are you honored?
That this segment
is for you?
Well then,
floss your teeth
with the pith!
Burst the pimples
with your tongue!

IV.
For the one I love
a crescent
that splinters
into a million jewels.
Pull down your sleeves!
Protect your palms
like fresh magnolia petals
from the embers,
their glow
pooling a buttery copper
in the corners of your eyes
in the creases on your forehead.

V.
Keep it for myself.
Keep it
deep
within me.

—*Giovanna Diaz*

Prose Poem

A prose poem, in its essence, is what it says it is: a "poem" written in prose form. It does not contain line breaks, mixes the qualities of prose and poetry, and makes use of the sentence. Prose poems have been a somewhat controversial genre, not perhaps in their content, but because of their genre title. Some poets and critics have been reluctant to accept the form into the larger category, reluctant to give it recognition for its poetic qualities. While the prose poem departs from verse in some ways, it indeed retains or re-creates poetic effect in other ways—and it certainly does not have the same nature as a narrative, essay, or short story. In his introduction to *Great American Prose Poems*, David Lehman says, "In verse, the tension between the line and the sentence can be fruitful. . . . The poet in prose must use the structure of the sentence itself, or the way one sentence modifies the next, to generate the surplus meaning that helps separate poetry in prose from ordinary writing" (22). He goes on to talk about antithesis, hesitation and reversal, and paradox as often giving life to prose poems, and also says that though the prose poem loses some abilities of the verse poem, it gains in "relaxation, in the possibilities of humor and incongruity, in narrative compression, and in the feeling of escape" (23).

Recommended Poem

Ginsberg, Allen. "A Supermarket in California." *Collected Poems 1947–1980*. Harper Perennial, 1988.

Recommended Books

Clements, Brian, and Jamey Dunham. *An Introduction to the Prose Poem*. Firewheel Editions, 2009.

Edson, Russell. *The Tunnel: Selected Poems*. Oberlin College Press, 1994.

Lehman, David, editor. *Great American Prose Poems: From Poe to the Present*. Scribner, 2003.

Ponge, Francis. *Soap*. Translated by Lane Dunlop. Stanford University Press, 1998.

Simic, Charles. *The World Doesn't End*. Harvest Books, 1989.

The Exercise

Write a prose poem. As well as finding content and imagery that offer tension, paradox, and antithesis, also craft sentences that do this—both within the sentence itself and between sentences. Don't forget to use punctuation, phrases and clauses, and any other sentence-building techniques to help achieve this end. While your prose poem may include a character or two, which would need to be supported with specific imagery, and may include the hint of a narrative, remember that a prose poem is not a short story with fully developed characters or plot. Its conflict is often found in the tensions, paradoxes, and antitheses found in the imagery colliding.

Example

Into

Some great long time ago, when there was nothing on earth but a church
in Spain, I was the rabbit in the moon and all the sandstorms and shadows
and people on earth fell away from my black curtain in monstrous clouds of
cosmic dust, great rusty vortexes of the stuff bringing fire and diamonds down
to the sea. In fact, that's what happened to Icarus. His wings did not melt and
betray him, but it was a burning diamond, uncut and perfect, flung down
from the sky that knocked him into the hungry tide.

—*Emma Burke*

Prose Poem in a Nonfiction or Alternate Form

Just as fiction can come in a nonfiction form, the prose poem need not be merely
a block of text. Prose poems can be created from various nonfiction forms—letters, instructions, or a series of aphorisms. Some forms might already be common to us; others writers could create themselves. Alternate "forms" for a prose
poem that are not a traditional prose poem nor a traditional nonfiction form
might include different types of lists, as can be seen in Richard Kostelanetz's
"First Truncated Epic," in Chris Murray's "Yao Ming's ABC of Basketball," and
in the student example below. Alternate forms of a prose poem would primarily
be informed by the beauty and grace of a prose sentence, possibly seen in isola-
tion (as with a list) and without the complication of line breaks or the volume of
a paragraph. Susan Briante's "Dear Mr. Chairman of the Federal Reserve Board"
serves as a fine example of a prose poem in the form of a letter. Her poem as
well as those by Kostelanetz and Murray can be found in the limited edition
literary journal *Sentence*, which featured prose poems of all types from around
the world.

Recommended Poems

Briante, Susan. "Dear Mr. Chairman of the Federal Reserve Board." *Sentence: A Journal of
Prose Poetics*, no. 3, 2005, pp. 169–70.

Kostelanetz, Richard. "First Truncated Epic." *Sentence: A Journal of Prose Poetics*, no. 5,
2007, pp. 216–20.

Murray, Chris. "Yao Ming's ABC of Basketball." *Sentence: A Journal of Prose Poetics*, no. 3,
2005, pp. 176–77.

The Exercise

Write a prose poem in the form of a letter, a series of instructions, a set of aphorisms, or a series of sentences that touch upon the main elements of something that is segmented. As with a prose poem, let tension, paradox, and antithesis arise from the images and grammatical structures in your poem.

Example

Come Home With . . .

I
All the letters I sent you

II
The freckle above your right brow

III
Wrinkled newspaper clippings from your jeans pocket

IV
Calloused palms

V
A half empty carton of cigarettes

VI
Your ukulele, my harmonica

VII
Time

—*Antonia Buban*

Line by Line

Forms can arise in relation to any part of a poem—sound, syllables, the line, stanzas, rhythm—or any combination. This exercise looks at what might happen when form arises from content itself: what if specific lines required specific content?

Though on the surface this exercise may seem overly prescriptive, it actually encourages some wilder associations and dramatic leaps between levels of consciousness, therefore freeing up the imagination from our tendencies toward strict logic. It also hones editing skills in the later stages of the exercise. As with any writing exercise, don't feel bound by each instruction; rather, use them as guidance and a jumping-off point.

The Exercise

Part 1. Write a poem using the following directions to create each line.

line 1: Describe the sky

line 2: Write more about the sky using a simile

line 3: Change your mind about the simile (why is it, after all, NOT like line 2?)

line 4: Describe something with a sound and a smell

line 5: Describe that same thing by how it feels to touch it

line 6: Write a line about you and a field and the night

line 7: Write a line telling how you feel with an image

line 8: Using the line above as a starting point, compare this feeling/image to something

line 9: Expand on this simile/metaphor/comparison

line 10: Write a line using a horse, the moon, and the ocean

line 11: Describe how it would feel to be in a fight (without using the word *fight*)

line 12: Describe paralysis (without using the words *paralyzed* or *move*)

line 13: Write a line using fire, a trumpet, and a wolf

line 14: Write a line using imagery from a dream

line 15: What if that dream became a nightmare? How would that image change?

line 16: What words would you speak to the nightmare image?

line 17: What force would you have move through the nightmare image?

line 18: End with the sky, echoing what you did in the first line, but modifying it slightly

Part 2. Revise the results until the poem is cohesive yet full of surprise and leaps every few lines. Feel free to rearrange, rewrite, add new line breaks, new stanzas, new images, and cut as much as needed to achieve a fully realized poem.

Example

Note that the following example will not necessarily match up perfectly line for line with Part 1 above, as it is the revised, edited version, but it is easy to see how Part 1 served as the genesis for many images.

Transcontinental Jam Jar

I had thought that smooth, outrageous blue
really spun at night, a spool of azure ribbon
(but it folded in my hands like a construction-paper square).
Scrape me together with rubber cement so that I
land softly on a warm pillow of freshly inked diaries,
falling through carpets and velvet and skies,
with the air pressing on my spindly limbs, crushing bones to ash.
Twist the lid shut, and turn me upside down so that I
collide with glass as you shake me,
silver light pulling pallid mares up from the sea and
crying out against the caress of brass knuckles
until blue blood thickens into minty toothpaste, cold.
Throw me to wolves as they wait for the fiery horizon's trumpet call
because the shimmering glow of a thousand street lamps
will bleed into neon police lights, flickering like
a broken open sign as I shout out the window for directions
since there is nowhere to go. Folding laminated maps
lay like blankets, covering cold skin but rendering us lost,
spinning under a paper-or-plastic indigo until we shatter on tile floors.

—*Caitlyn Le*

Poetry Aphorism

The thought that poetry contains wisdom, even a power to protect or heal our psyche, should lead us to the idea that wisdom about poetry could be just as powerful. Wisdom about poetry comes in many forms, from essays to poems about poetry. The aphorism, a statement that by its nature contains a wise observation, serves as one of the most effective forms to encourage this discovery. The aphoristic statement about poetry can do much more than inform and can be like the line or fragment of a poem itself.

Recommended Book

Ferlinghetti, Lawrence. *Poetry as Insurgent Art*. New Directions, 2007. Here, Ferlinghetti offers an entire book of poetry aphorisms.

The Exercise

Write an aphorism about what poetry is or what it means to be a poet. An aphorism is best kept short, usually one sentence, at most two, but carefully crafted, packed tightly with powerful word choice. An aphorism may contain one central image, or it may simply discuss an idea in abstract, philosophical terms.

Examples

> Poetry is looking at an oak tree and saying "look, it's a priest made of cornbread!" and making everyone realize they've never seen an oak tree before in its real light. And then at night with cornbread on their kitchen table, everyone chews on impossible truths.
>
> —*Tory Tarpley*

> Poetry is the ritualistic knitting of the collective unconscious into a holy book that continually reconsiders the mysticism of being alive.
>
> —*Madeline Burch*

Imitation of Form

Imitations are one of the old standbys in practicing one's art. Many basic Creative Writing courses have used the imitation to instruct, and poets have sometimes paid homage to those who have influenced them through imitation. Much can be learned from an imitation, but there are many dangers, too. One can easily get stuck inside someone else's voice or style. One of my favorite phrases to quote to students when they become overwhelmed with "who to sound like" after they have read much good material is "the anxiety of influence."

To avoid the "anxiety of influence" and to guide the practice of imitation to a tangible result, it's best to choose something specific to imitate. While there could be many elements in a poem to imitate, from philosophical perspective to style of imagery, this exercise encourages you to retain your own perspective and imagery and allow them to be shaped by imitating another author's form. While form does not represent the purpose of the poem, it certainly is a major component of style and can help shape meaning. For the purposes of this exercise, look for forms created by authors specifically for a particular poem (through patterns of grammar, word choice, call and response, etc.) rather than formal genre-wide forms such as sonnets or haiku.

The Exercise

Find a poem that seems structured by a form particular to that poem—one in which a pattern, such as a pattern of grammar, word choice, call and response, etc., gives shape to the images, ideas, and voice (or voices) in the poem. Choose any poem that you know of and love that fits these parameters. If needed, check out some of the recommended poems below. Write your own poem following the structure of your chosen poem, supplying your own ideas and images. Don't be afraid to alter the form slightly, though with any alteration give attention to consistency and how those alterations may impact meaning. Also, when writing an imitation, it is customary to indicate the poet or poem imitated by writing "after [poem or poet's name]" just after your own title.

Recommended Poems

Bell, Marvin. "In." *Drawn by Stones, by Earth, by Things That Have Been in the Fire*. Atheneum, 1984. Bell uses parallel structure (repeatedly beginning his sentences with "In" to create a song-like or chant-like form for the poem).

Lorca, Federico García. "Lament for Ignacio Sánchez Mejías." *Collected Poems*. Translated by Christopher Maurer. Farrar, Straus, and Giroux, 2002. In this poem, Lorca uses the refrain of "at five in the afternoon" repeatedly throughout to build the emotional weight surrounding the death of Mejias.

Paz, Octavio. "Duration." *The Collected Poems of Octavio Paz: 1957–1987*. Edited by Eliot Weinberger. New Directions, 1991. In this poem, Paz plays with the call and response form.

Example

Repuesta
(after "Duration" by Octavio Paz)

I will ride to you in a chariot of threads
(answer with a scissor-blade embrace)

I will break apart your night-soaked necklace
(answer with a stream of burnt pearls)

I will strum to wake tides of a sleeping sea
(answer with a bridge of sand-wrinkled rocks)

I will whisper bone shards against the walls
(answer with a mask of porcelain wind)

I will climb the lips of a dusty lock
(answer with cords of shattered wine)

—*Patricia Lee*

Found Poem

Jack Myers's *Dictionary of Poetic Terms* defines a found poem as

> a piece of writing that, without change in its conception or major reorganization or substantial distortion, could be considered a poem. Usually, the found poem is wrested from a mundane domain (street signs, business notices, newspaper advertisements) and isolated so that it takes on an ironic, dramatic, or multilayered meaning. (142)

Though not much writing is involved when one presents a found poem, it requires much in terms of vision. The complexities, the depths, the associations, the ramifications of things that might be mundane on one level, philosophical on another, burst forth in the found poem. Found poetry can also be a great place for satire, as has been done by taking quotes by politicians and celebrities and placing them in "poetic" context.

Recommended Poems

Gross, Ronald. "Thank You—Come Again" and "Ice Cream Cone." *Pop Poems*. Simon and Schuster, 1967. In "Thank You—Come Again," Gross uses the found language of commercial signage to comment on materialism's impact on human interactions. In "Ice Cream Cone," he simply lists the ingredients of the cone, eliciting reflection on the unknown foods and chemicals we put in our bodies.

Recommended Books

Petras, Kathryn, and Ross Petras. *The Anthology of Really Important Modern Poetry: Timeless Poems by Snooki, John Boehner, Kanye West, and Other Well-Versed Celebrities*. Workman Publishing Company, 2012.

Seely, Hart. *Pieces of Intelligence: The Existential Poetry of Donald H. Rumsfeld*. Free Press, 2009. Seely presents quotes from former Secretary of Defense Rumsfeld in poetic fashion.

The Exercise

"Find" a poem. Look everywhere—packages, television, on the ground, in the newspaper, in the tabloids, signs, instruction booklets—look anywhere and everywhere. Give the poem a title, one that deepens its meaning, and present it in a way (line breaks? one-line poem? visual poem?) that would heighten our awareness of the poignancy of the words and content. The title and the physical format that you supply should greatly shape our perception of the original text.

Example

The Night Before

Windows has
encountered a problem
and needs to be
shut down.

—Vivian Ludford

Coinage

Language is not static. Either over time or at the hands of an author who has a specific purpose, language can dynamically shift in spelling, capitalization, usage, part of speech, form, and so on. New words can be coined altogether, or they can be formed from root words. Compound words often seem to be used in humorous or satirical contexts, but they can have serious purpose, too—Paul Celan, Holocaust survivor and poet, used many compound words in his poems to reflect the colliding, violent, dualistic world he saw around him.

The Exercises

This exercise begins with the same task but can be executed in two different formats. Initial step: take two words that would normally be unrelated and think of what imaginatively might be created if these things were put together. Then complete one or both of the following.

1. Write a poem in the form of a definition and etymology.
2. Write a narrative poem that serves as an example of your coined word.

Example

fellwell

overtaken by the weight of my
backpack, i fall down the stairs, head first.
newly tightened braces cut my upper
lip, knees skin with rug burn.
i swipe a finger at my nose, and the blood comes.
passersby become witnesses, with questions
only i can answer. mostly over text
do i tell people that i'm okay,
and remembering the
nurse's incident
report, that i
fellwell.

—*Emily Nielson*

Epic Lists

In the great epics, poets often used lists not only to offer details themselves, but also to create a sense of grandness, or epic-ness, if you will. Epic lists (sometimes also called epic catalogues) might have been simple in some cases (lists of beautiful women and goddesses) or they may have been aimed at stirring the senses (lists of food and drink consumed at a banquet). This exercise encourages a writer to consider a number of things that could possibly be or become an epic list.

One of my favorite examples of a list that becomes epic with some attention to language is found, of all places, not in literature but in the world of entomology. Justin O. Schmidt, researcher at the Carl Hayden Bee Research Center, is the creator of the Schmidt Pain Scale for Stinging Insects. Schmidt sought in his ratings of the pain caused by insect stings to communicate a deep understanding of what the stings felt like, so he turned to the language of poetry to do so, crafting metaphors for each of the stings he has experienced. The language that Schmidt uses makes even a bee sting seem beautiful in a way! If one were to consider a purpose for such a list or catalog, it's fairly easy to see that Schmidt's descriptive presentation of his information communicates, celebrates, and creates awareness and interest. Do think of purpose as you consider the epic list. An epic list is usually grand and growing in nature, even as it looks at smaller and smaller details. An epic list seeks to expand your awareness. An epic list can be beautiful, serious, humorous, and especially satirical. *McSweeney's Internet Tendency* contains a great repository of satirical lists.

Recommended Article

Young, Lauren. "Ranking the Pain of Stinging Insects, from 'Caustic' to 'Blinding.'" *Atlas Obscura*, 20 June 2016, www.atlasobscura.com/articles/the-colorful-pain-index-of-the-stinging-ants-bees-and-wasps-around-the-world. Young's article features the Schmidt Pain Scale in full.

Recommended Website

Lists at *McSweeney's*: www.mcsweeneys.net/columns/lists

The Exercise

Write an "epic list" poem. Consider your purpose and how your language and the format of the list can support your purpose. Let the list expand and use vocabulary, syntax, imagery, and literary devices that show us an entire world, whether that be macroscopic or microscopic.

Example

Babel

Russian—ornate jewels that roll across the tongue, thick like dark chocolate.

German—thin flakes that fall from crisp phyllo dough onto an off-white plate, a sprig of mint, and a toothpick.

French—a mixture between hushed, conspiring voices and brass horns in the countryside.

Japanese—like sucking on sugarcane stalks in the summer, like running along finished wood, like colliding two coconut halves.

Spanish—the clicks from tap shoes and midnight lightning dances.

Italian—wild horse mane billowing blooming and ripping holes in the wind. Tastes like gems of caviar.

American English—loosely bound yarn, yellow from the sun, smells like a green field with pollen, makes you sneeze.

British English—embroidered satin lined with lace. The loose threads are cut.

Chinese—shrieking birds, rumbling impasses, a single thread of song.

—*Katharine Lin*

Beatitudes

Even for those not of the Christian faith, Jesus's statements often referred to as the Beatitudes are considered some of the most noble sayings ever spoken. Their empathy and wisdom seem to defy the realities of the world to the point of paradox, especially with statements such as "Blessed are the meek, for they shall inherit the earth." The word *beatitude* means "great happiness." As Jesus talks about the meek and the poor in spirit and envisions a world of happiness for them, his words take on both a prophetic and a poetic tone. The parallelism, the expansiveness, the wisdom, and the imagery that all burst forth from these statements have inspired both the religious and the nonreligious for centuries. Even the Beat Generation found great inspiration in these words, possibly taking the name of their movement from Jesus's words, though there is still debate about the origin of their name.

Beyond Jesus, others have written such statements of wisdom. Anne Sexton's poem "First Psalm" is a fine example. The Beatitudes use a refrain of "Blessed are . . ." and Sexton uses the similar phrase "Let there be . . ." to introduce her images. Like the Beatitudes, Sexton uses parallelism and imagery to create an incantation of sorts.

Recommended Texts

Matthew 5:1–12. *The Bible*. English Standard Version. Crossway, 2007.

Sexton, Anne. "First Psalm." *The Complete Poems*. Mariner Books, 1999.

The Exercise

In the form of a poem or a series of sentence-statements, write your own statements of wisdom, empathy, positivity, possibility, genesis, or any such noble state. Use an opening tag such as "Blessed be . . ." or "Let there be . . ." or "Let the . . ." or "Praise be . . ." or any other positive, inviting opening phrase you can think of. Let the piece be rich in imagery and attentive to rhythm.

Example

Blessed Be

Blessed be the lotus that blooms alone in winter
The delicate petals wrapped in silence
Protected from the harsh world if only
For a moment

Blessed be the pocket watch chain intertwining at its roots
Forgoing time and suspending
The brittleness of life
In a bubble of air to breathe
Warmth upon its body

Blessed be the prior lives beneath its weight
To hold its heavy leaves
For it may die soon, but it had the strength
To break into a place another dared not go
A frozen curiosity
So perhaps it will live on after all
If only in a memory of a dream
It will remain

—*Caitlyn Shannon*

Tiny Poem

The tiny poem has an immense power. It is expansive. It is microscopic. It sees both the thing and the everything.

Robert Bly's seminal anthology *The Sea and the Honeycomb* explores the art of the tiny poem. "Most of the emotions we have are brief," Bly says in the introduction. "They are part of the swift life on the intelligence" (5). Bly goes on to recognize the importance of sensitivity in composing such poems, a sensitivity that includes rather than excludes, perhaps a paradox considering the brevity of tiny poems. According to Bly, we must recognize and include such brief emotions to fully understand the human being.

A tiny poem is not about exclusion. It is about focus, about an intense burst, about a singularity or a duplicity or duality. A tiny poem is not suppressive. But a tiny poem is attentive to the primary—the primary image, the primary thought. Bly says, "[A] brief poem does without the scaffolding of secondary ideas" (6).

Bly describes both the "intellectual exhilaration" of the tiny poem and the risk. The poet does not, through words, remain hanging around to prop up the reader. Bly suggests that readers with "strong imaginations" (6) will most enjoy a tiny poem. In this sense, a tiny poem can require, on the part of both the writer and the reader, a greater sense of concentration than is required with a longer poem.

What defines a tiny poem? There are some forms based on brevity: the haiku, the landay, the sijo, the tanka. Even the one-line poem, though not necessarily a "form," definitely can be described in terms of what facets make it effective or not. Bly suggests, and most would agree, that the sonnet is much too long to be considered a tiny poem. "Tiny" poems are usually only a few lines long.

Tiny poems need not adhere to a recognized poetic form, though. There are many tiny poems, both classic and contemporary, that are not haiku. However, for tiny poems to work well, especially if they do not follow a preset pattern, they do need to create their own form, in a sense. Much of that success lies with the grammatical forms used and with the line breaks. For example, a poem just four lines long that seeks to say something specific and significant must work within a tight grammatical structure, letting phrases and clauses (or sometimes just one such grammatical unit) bear some of the weight of building a relationship between elements in the poem. Likewise, line breaks should be used to create tension and surprise, making these few lines affecting rather than dismissible.

Recommended Book

Bly, Robert, editor. *The Sea and the Honeycomb: A Book of Poems*. Sixties Press, 1966. While Bly's entire anthology consists of tiny poems, I particularly recommend Salvatore Quasimodo's "And Suddenly It's Evening," D. H. Lawrence's "The White Horse," Guillaume Apollinaire's "The Owl," Jorge Carrera Andrade's "Walnut," and René Char's "The Oriole."

The Exercise

Write a tiny poem, four to six lines long, that relies not on form but on its singular vision and idea (whether that be microscopic or macrocosmic); its imagery (one or two or just a handful); and its carefully wrought wording. What interplay might there be between an image or two and one moment of exposition? What interplay might arise from juxtaposing two images? In terms of the grammatical structure of the poem, to encourage concision and relationship, consider making the entire poem just one sentence long. This will also encourage more effective line breaks.

Example

Iceberg

Weak like dying oak
peel me like lettuce
and review my potential
before throwing me into the emerald bowl

—*Ash Chen*

Monostich: The One-Line Poem

I believe strongly in the power of a small poem, and the one-line poem (also known as the monostich) stands as the zenith of this kind of brief, bursting expression. A one-line poem has an expansive power, and, after reading one, we are left with a kind of echoing. When I think of what happens after a one-line poem, I think of the silence that echoes in a room someone has just exited or the echoes that resonate in the pauses in the Beach Boys' "Good Vibrations." The power of a one-line poem is positive, whatever the content. There is something thrilling and even hopeful that so few words could hold so much meaning. Once I remarked to a class that "brevity is optimism." That is, believing in your words so strongly, believing that other human beings will care about and be moved by just a handful of words, is optimistic. In the *Dictionary of Poetic Terms*, Jack Myers says that the one-line poem has "succinctness, grace, thrust, and penetration" (233).

A one-line poem is not easy to write. It is not an unfinished poem, but a specific door of possibility, sometimes even an entire world, all within a hand-held space. In his *Writer's Chronicle* article "One-Line Poems: The Smallest Talk," Michael McFee says, "[I]t's a self-contained verbal world from which not a word can be shaken, and to which not a word should be added" (66).

McFee notes other qualities of the one-line poem: lyric, subversive, wise (rather than clever), and intense in diction and rhythm. Of a one-line poem's lyricism he says, "[A] one-line poem is not a kind of maxim or aphorism or Zen adage. It is, like all lyric poems, a showing and not a saying" (68). He notes the importance of a one-line poem's title and that the poem depends on the title to work: "[I]t's the crucial initial note in the chord struck by the poem" (67).

Recommended Article

McFee, Michael. "One-Line Poems: The Smallest Talk." *Writer's Chronicle*, vol. 40, no. 4, Feb. 2008, pp. 66–68.

Recommended Book

Matthews, William. *An Oar in the Old Water*. The Stone, 1979. Every poem in Matthews's book is a one-line poem. I particularly recommend "Her Name," "The Same Dream," "Night," and "Sleep."

The Exercise

Write a one-line poem. Rather than writing an aphoristic, advice-like statement, let an image or two, complicated by some juxtaposition, twist of detail, or subtle addition of a surprising word or two, carry the poem. Title it in a way that gives the poem some context or creates some tension.

Examples

Sandstorm

Speed into my tent with hurricane intensity cradling 7566 miles of longing

—*Alex Queener*

Pinwheels

You still have me cartwheeling to nowhere.

—*Caitlyn Le*

Unrelenting Question

How do we get over, under, and behind the fence?

—*Taylor Dilbeck*

Video Games

Right after I save the princess, again.

—*Caroline Mullens*

Two-Line Poem

This exercise is much like the one-line poem, but the second line, as well as a line-break, can add a layer of complexity, shift the tone of the poem, or reposition it into a completely different level of consciousness. That line break, coupled with enjambment, can create a nice surprise. At other times, the line break with an end-stop simply allows the poem to push into a deeper, inner space . . . or even outward into the grand, sweeping world beyond.

Recommended Poems

Goldbarth, Albert. "Birds." *To Be Read in 500 Years*. Graywolf Press, 2009.

Yakich, Mark. "Before Losing Yourself Completely to Love." *Unrelated Individuals Forming a Group Waiting to Cross*. Penguin Books, 2004.

The Exercise

Write a two-line poem. With the second line, work for surprise or complexity. That line might shift the tone of the poem, might resolve a tension in the first line, or might create an unresolved tension. The line break may contain enjambment or not, but should be crafted to aid the purpose of the two lines.

Example

At the County Fair in October

The carney with broken teeth asked if I was your wife,
you said yes.

—Peyton Budd

One-Word Poem

In his article on one-line poetry, "One-Line Poems: The Smallest Talk," Michael McFee wonders if a one-word poem is possible. Poems are already quite condensed, but can one word carry not only its connotative value, but also a sense of complex image or perhaps narrative?

I like to first explore the power of one word by thinking about distilling a poem into first a favorite line, and then down into a favorite word. You could use any poem, but I like to use Allen Ginsberg's "A Supermarket in California." I've often been surprised at how differently students respond, how often they choose different words from each other when I ask what one word is most important in the poem. Almost none of them agree! Then, prompted by their thoughts of what words would be evocative and provocative, I ask students to write a one-word poem. I do let them, and ask them, to provide a title, and I let them make the title however long they wish.

The Exercise

Write a one-word poem. Don't necessarily go for a big, academic-sounding word, or rely on the emotionally manipulative nature of a word. Use the title, if you need to, to provide context.

Example

The Psychopath

Mosquito

—Margaret Hardage

Circular Poem

Visual texts, including visual poetry, are not by any means a modern invention. Though the rising popularity of comics and graphic novels has given way to their more recent inclusion in the classroom, visual texts—from the Egyptian Book of the Dead to medieval illuminated manuscripts to William Blake—have been around since the advent of literature. And while some visual poets use traditional mediums (pen and paper, paint, typewriters), others have turned to modern technology (Photoshop, video). Visual poetry comes in many forms: concrete poetry (poetry that takes on the shape of its subject); comics poetry (see the collaboration between Josh Neufeld and Nick Flynn for Flynn's poem "Cartoon Physics, Part I"); word art (which blurs the line between poetry and visual art); and video poetry (Button Poetry has a stunning YouTube channel that features many poets reading, sometimes in a short-film-style format).

Concrete poetry is often popular with young children, and while there are well-done concrete poems out there, I confess that many seem too simplistic (for example, a poem about a diamond in the shape of a diamond). This exercise brings together the structure of the poem with the structure of the visual element, but requires not that the topic match the shape, but that the wording of the poem work as the shape does.

The Exercise

Write a poem that will read and can be presented in a circular fashion. Think about how parts of speech, especially prepositions or participles, might help a sentence loop around continuously. Physically write or design your poem as a circle. While some may simply do this with pen and paper, others may want to experiment with available technology to learn how to design their poem digitally. The poem may stand on its own without a title, or, if you do offer a title, it may need to stand separately from the circle to differentiate it from the rest of the text.

Example

Ace of Hearts

—Keaten Olson

Create Your Own Form

Giving shape to our emotions and ideas is profoundly important if they are to become a poem. Even in free verse, poets must make decisions about how their words will take shape. At times it is best to write freely, then shape and edit later. But it can be helpful and even fun to create the form and then write according to those specifications.

The Exercise

Create your own form for a poem, and then write such a poem. Think about these things as you decide what form to create:

- The elements of a poem: imagery, figurative language, lines, stanzas, sections
- Grammatical elements: parts of speech, connotation and denotation, phrases and clauses, parallel structure, syllables
- Patterns: patterns with grammar, imagery, or other poetic elements
- Sound: rhythm, sound devices (consonance, assonance), tone
- Numerical possibilities: number of words or syllables in a particular space, increasing or decreasing numbers of elements in a particular space
- Forms from outside of poetry: lab reports, timelines, legal briefs, footnotes

Example

Now it's your turn!

Last Thunder: Final Thoughts and Essays

Leaping Poetry: Writing on Multiple Levels of Consciousness

Throughout these writing exercises, numerous techniques (such as synesthesia or layering a metaphor) draw from what Robert Bly terms *leaping poetry,* that is, poetry that relies on multiple levels of consciousness, attempting to make two disparate worlds one (such as the intangible and the tangible). When we speak of levels of consciousness, what does this mean? Though they are not the only forms of consciousness, just think of the difference between the conscious world (our daily, waking life), the subconscious world (our unrealized thoughts or primal emotions), and the unconscious world (our sleep). A "leap" occurs when a work of art, poetry in this case, jumps from one level to another or brings two or more together in metaphor, juxtaposition, or some other method.

Our adult lives require us to be so practical that we often neglect the other parts of our consciousness. Many would agree that our imaginations die as we grow older and become diluted by our daily lives. Surely, the conscious life is important and is essential for navigating reality and communicating clearly, but it is often in operating within the other levels (the figurative, the unconscious, the subconscious, and for some, the super-conscious [such as Emerson's Over-Soul]) that we navigate our inner lives and communicate and connect more deeply. Writing poetry, which is the language art most in direct contact with the inner life, is a fantastic way to maintain imagination and its power to connect what is within to what is without. In addition to thinking about levels of consciousness, such as the conscious, subconscious, and unconscious, these realms can also be thought of in terms of things that are imagined versus real, tangible versus intangible, present versus removed or imagined, or in terms of the concepts of dualism, such as heaven and earth, the soul and the body, emotions and logic, and so on. While some philosophical systems such as Plato's Theory of Forms, some religious beliefs such as Gnosticism, and even some literary movements such as the Enlightenment argue for a separation of these "levels," most poetry, from the mythological poems written by Enheduanna in 2300 BCE to the surrealist poetry of contemporary literature, seeks to unite these things—manifesting, in the form of words, how two worlds can be made one.

Artists throughout the ages have tried many methods to access and operate within those levels: meditation, prayer, the use of music, communing with nature, exercise (think of Wordsworth's brisk walks through the Lake District), and psychic or surrealist automatism (a method used by surrealist and abstract artists). There are also a number of techniques that assist in making a leap between levels of consciousness or that represent leaps in and of themselves, particularly stream-of-consciousness writing, metaphor, and juxtaposition.

Stream-of-consciousness writing aims to produce thoughts and imagery that arise from a deeper level of consciousness—writing that is not a product of our most easily accessible, perhaps even clichéd thoughts—by having the writer compose without stopping and without worrying about typical conventions such as grammatical rules. The uninterrupted speed and freedom that a writer feels in this process should result in something transcendent.

Metaphor is a technique that is a leap in and of itself. When one begins with a tenor (the initial, main image or idea that a writer is describing) and proceeds in comparison to the vehicle (the portion of the metaphor that the initial image or idea is compared to), there must be a leap. There is a leap from the tenor, which is usually literally present in the context of the poem, to the vehicle, which is usually not present (it is elsewhere or perhaps even merely imagined). There is also a leap from the tenor to the vehicle in the sense that, though they share one commonality that serves as the "ground" for their comparison, the metaphor must leap over all of the ground that they do not share. Tenors and vehicles cannot be similar in too many regards or they do not qualify as metaphor. "My house is like your house" is not a metaphor. Juxtaposition works in this same way, perhaps in an even more sudden way since it presents a collision of images without transition or explicit explanation of relationship.

The leap can be experienced in a multitude of ways: long and floating, gradual, short, singular, multiple. It might be gentle or fragmented or any combination. It might be an association or an illogical fusion. It offers surprise and depth and intensity. And though there are techniques that embody or achieve leaps, what is most important to understand is that, as Robert Bly teaches, leaping or writing on multiple levels of consciousness is not a technique but an awareness.

Speaking of writing on multiple levels of consciousness might bring to mind thoughts of highly obtuse poems with private symbolism that an author can feel their way through, but not necessarily a reader. This does not have to be so. In fact, Wordsworth and Coleridge were interested in expressing these deep matters, the inner self of the common man, in common language. One can find much direct commentary about operating on multiple levels of consciousness in the poetry and prose of the Romantics and the Transcendentalists: the preface to *Lyrical Ballads* and its discussion of the primacy of the imagination, Thoreau's transcendent experiences in *Walden*. Other writers, particularly forward-thinking writers of the twentieth and twenty-first centuries, have allowed their style to begin to mimic the thought patterns of leaping between levels of consciousness. Some of these forms do present poetry in a more challenging way, such as with surrealism. But keep in mind that, even within the most illogical writings of surrealism, the goal of the author is never to confuse a reader—they may want to astound a reader so as to shock them out of their normal mode of thought in order to reach deeper, but they do not create a purposeless maze. The Spanish-language poets and fiction writers do it particularly well: the poems of Lorca, the magical realism of Márquez. Those writers are deeply ingrained in their respective cultures, widely read there and felt to be widely accessible.

Perhaps a key feature of poetry itself is that it indeed leaps between the author and the audience, between the self and others, though mainly when we speak of leaping poetry or poetry that operates on multiple levels of consciousness, we are speaking of matters such as the subconscious or unconscious mind, something that begins on a very personal level. Leaping between levels of consciousness certainly provides much opportunity for surprise in language and structure, but its ultimate goal is to provide the surprise that travels out from the page, in to the reader in a deep place, and then outward again as that reader expresses the "aha" moment. Mostly, understanding writing in this way is about a vision, one that understands the dream-like and associative properties of the human mind and of imagery.

For an exercise that encourages leaps in levels of consciousness as well as a student poem that serves as a fine example, see the "Layering a Metaphor" exercise and An Rhiel Wang's "At My Old House" in Chapter 2. Also consider trying your hand at these exercises, all of which encourage leaps in a variety of ways: "Synesthesia," "Making a Poem Turn Up or Down," "Transcendental Imagery," "Shifting Image," "Enantiodromia," and "Epistrophy" (all Chapter 2).

For further prose reading on the subject and for professional examples, read Robert Bly's anthologies *Leaping Poetry* and *News of the Universe: Poems of Twofold Consciousness*.

Recommended Books

Bly, Robert. *Leaping Poetry: An Idea with Poems and Translations*. University of Pittsburgh Press, 2008.

Bly, Robert, editor. *News of the Universe: Poems of Twofold Consciousness*. Counterpoint, 2015.

The Oulipo Society: Constrained Writing and Adapting These Exercises

The Oulipo Society was a twentieth-century French literary movement that tasked its members with constrained writing. Constrained writing is a technique that requires some pattern or forbids an element of language, all with the goal of pushing language into fresh, unfamiliar territory rather than it following territory already carved out by previous tradition. While constrained writing might seem punishingly limiting, it ultimately leads to better practice in technique and greater freedom (think of the freedom of flight being facilitated by the rules and constraints of aerodynamics and the engineering of aircraft).

Here are some typical techniques used in constrained writing: lipogram (where a certain letter, such as an *e*, is not allowed to be used anywhere in the piece); a reverse lipogram (where a certain letter must be used); the prescribed use of palindromes or other required vocabulary; chaterism (where each word grows larger or smaller in length); and, similar to chaterism, the intentional increase or decrease in syllable or letter count.

Whenever I have tasked my students with constrained writing, the response is usually terror and incredulity—at first. During the process, they often say that it is the hardest piece they have ever written. But afterwards, they are always exhilarated by the process; and, even when not, always proud of the quality of the final product, definitely interested in it and instructed by it. And I would say that, although there are certainly exceptions, there are many cases in which constrained writing produces some of my students' best work. For there is no other time at which they give so close attention to each word, each syllable, each letter. We all know the practice of close reading—constrained writing is close writing.

While it may seem an antithetical approach in a book designed to foster the wild, unpredictable nature of lightning in writing, to stir the imagination, and to cultivate imagination and freedom, I would argue that, in the right way and at the right time, constrained writing can be a path to such freedoms.

I encourage the adaptation of the exercises in this book—break the rules, use them as a beginning point, combine them, and, by all means, add some of the techniques of constrained writing to complicate them. As always, write freely first, then edit based on the parameters, for writing from the spirit of genesis, the spark of the idea, is the ultimate heart of what you will do as a writer. But don't stop there—give your work shape, give it attention, and nurture it as you would a child!

Final Words for Teachers

I sincerely hope and believe that these poetry writing exercises can and will help electrify your classroom. Built into these exercises is the belief that inspiration, vision, and a path forward as a writer are just as important as the technique itself. Many years ago, one of my Creative Writing students, halfway through the first semester, suddenly remarked that she finally understood what I was trying to do: "You don't just want us to be better writers; you want us to evolve!" She did get it, though of course the two go hand in hand.

I also hope that you will go beyond these exercises and even create your own along these lines. Most of these exercises were, in a general sense, reverse engineered from readings and experiences I have had as a poet. Where did James Wright come up with the imagery for his poem "The Jewel?" How can the imagery in Anne Sexton's poem "The Fury of Overshoes" seem so simple, yet have such a deep, echoing emotional impact? What relationship can science and poetry have? Is a form like the landay restrictive or freeing? These kinds of questions that I encountered as I read and wrote led me to these exercises. As you read poetry, work backwards and ask yourself what images, emotions, and experiences led the poet down that path.

Experience as a writer has been invaluable to me as a teacher of writing. Just as you use these exercises for your students, I hope that you, too, will try them. In fact, to create the full experience for your students, I would argue that a teacher writing along with his or her students is just as crucial as any amount of academic knowledge. Being a part of a community of writers in the classroom is, without a doubt, the most effective (and fun) way for students to achieve growth as writers, and it is always more effective if teachers show that they are learning and working, too, and making themselves vulnerable just as the students are.

Creating a community of writers in the classroom takes lots of delicate work on the part of the teacher, and I find that work to be a bit different with each different group of students. Some groups come in as average or reluctant writers; some come in as self-professed poets or novelists of the future. But if either group doesn't trust each other, the results can be painful. In both cases—with weak writers and strong—the best classroom writing experiences come when the students trust each other, respect each other's work, and view the teacher as a participant in the work and learning.

In my classes, I employ a number of methods to create a stronger community. Chief among those methods is to waste a little time—time for jokes, current events discussions, rants, emotional check-ins, movie reviews, listening to a new song, hearing about their weekend events, letting students tell stories from their lives. All the while, I understand that students are expressing themselves and thus, yes, *telling their stories*. And in the back of my mind, I might even be looking for connections in the things that we read or write. In truth, I don't feel that there are any "off topic" conversations in English. At the very least, we are learning to listen to others.

The workshop approach is the most definable key method in a community of writers. It is the hallmark of postsecondary writing programs, so it needs little introduction or explanation. I would note a few things about the workshops I run in class. While most students fear hearing negative critiques, most often the problems center on critiques that are too nice. I spend a week or two building up to the "improvement" critiques so that we create some trust and goodwill in the classroom. Beyond that, I find that the thing I most often have to prompt or coax out of the students is what they would suggest for improvements in the piece we are reviewing. Most often, I ask that the student writer reads their own work aloud for the class. This gives them ownership, voice, agency, and usually results in the most accurate emotional reading. And while it creates nerves, in the end, it more so creates confidence. There are other times, though, when we read pieces anonymously, which alters the experience for both writer and audience. Most often critiques are delivered through class discussion, though there are times we write them out. Sometimes we write a critique sitting silently and pass them anonymously to the writer; other times we create "critique stations" where students move from printed poem to printed poem to add notes. I also spend lots of time, over the course of the semester or year, training students in what to notice in a poem, what to ask about it, what to comment on, and what a hierarchy of concerns looks like: spelling is less important, the image utmost.

Without a doubt, the workshop method and the community in the classroom are the best educators for teaching audience. And an awareness and understanding of audience is so much of what drives great writing. I teach my students that audience, especially in poetry, is often not as much about a particular group of people, but more about a part, often emotional, of all people. We practice and learn to watch for this in our interactions and work in the classroom. We discuss audience reactions, and the workshop method allows us a lab to see it in real time.

Most of all, the most successful writing classrooms are the ones wherein a safe space and challenge are balanced in a way that energizes students. Students increasingly need space and time that allow them to explore and express their feelings, experiences, and questions. And they need us to guide and challenge them to make something beautiful and positive out of a world that can often answer their questions with storm.

Final Words for Writers

Words are waiting to be discovered because the world is waiting to be discovered. And like words, that world is not one thing, but many at once. To navigate ourselves through what is created and what is destroyed, through what is glorious and what is poisonous, through what is felt and what is received, through what is hoped for and what is lived, we need to be able to observe, to recognize, to categorize, to reorder, to imagine, to sing, to praise, to mourn, to name, and to communicate. And in naming and communicating, to write. To paraphrase Samuel Taylor Coleridge, we must discover the best words and discover their best order. In so doing, we make a world, through at least meaning if not through material. You must ask and investigate what your vision of the world is and whether it flows out of a passive, flailing reaction to experience or out of your power to experience, think, feel, question, rethink, align, realign, remember, disquiet, disrupt, disorganize, form, and specify. And, very important, to empathize. When we do these things with words, we are participating in an ascension to a unified vision of humanity and the universe, one that binds the relationships in language to the relationships of creation.

And yes, words are waiting to be created, too. Words aren't so much discovered within ourselves—sometimes they are—but are a part of human connection and communication. Maybe we've forgotten certain words, or an order to the words ignites some feeling, memory, or idea that has been latent. We shape sounds, make meaning, give tangible form to things intangible. We pair those sounds and abstract shapes that we call letters with experiences and call it language. And we must find a way to familiarize our language with the language of others—communication, interpretation, synthesis, translation. And this is where, however much we have created language in and of ourselves and for ourselves and by ourselves, we must discover something. Discover what words mean to others. And why. And why it matters. We must discover other lives.

To write well, to extend your abilities beyond these exercises, live. Explore. Travel. Listen. Gather stories. Look someone in the eyes. Ask questions. Begin with someone as far from you as possible—different gender, different age, different culture, different values. Work back toward yourself and, in years, you will find someone different from the self that began on that path.

The image, the line, the music, the metaphor, the poem—these are our powers to make these lightning paths. The speed, the heat, the force, the ability to create or destroy. The danger! What will you say and where will it strike? Its light might blind and burn, will be brilliant. It will fork this way and that, rise up, rain down, send shock waves far beyond where it is seen. Poetry is a lightning path—unforgettable, transformational.

Finally, I also hope that you will consult these fine resources that taught me so much about poetry:

Ali, Kazim. *Orange Alert: Essays on Poetry, Art, and the Architecture of Silence*. University of Michigan Press, 2010.

Berg, Stephen, editor. *My Business Is Circumference: Poets on Influence and Mastery*. Paul Dry Books, 2001.

Bly, Robert. *Talking All Morning*. University of Michigan Press, 1980.

Hall, Donald, editor. *Claims for Poetry*. University of Michigan Press, 1982.

Hugo, Richard. *The Triggering Town: Lectures and Essays on Poetry and Writing*. W. W. Norton & Company, 2010.

Koch, Kenneth. *Making Your Own Days: The Pleasures of Reading and Writing Poetry*. Scribner, 1998.

Levertov, Denise. *The Poet in the World*. New Directions, 1973.

Lorca, Federico García. *In Search of Duende*. Translated by Christopher Maurer. New Directions, 2010.

Mattawa, Khaled. *How Long Have You Been With Us?: Essays on Poetry*. University of Michigan Press, 2016.

Muske, Carol. *Women and Poetry: Truth, Autobiography, and the Shape of the Self*. University of Michigan Press, 1997.

Myers, Jack. *The Portable Poetry Workshop*. Heinle Publishers, 2004.

Myers, Jack, and Don C. Wukasch. *Dictionary of Poetic Terms*. University of North Texas Press, 2003.

Orr, Gregory. *Poetry as Survival*. University of Georgia Press, 2002.

Rilke, Rainer Maria. *Letters to a Young Poet*. Translated by M. D. Herter Norton. W. W. Norton & Company, 1993.

Roethke, Theodore. *On Poetry & Craft*. Copper Canyon Press, 2001.

Simic, Charles. *The Metaphysician in the Dark*. University of Michigan Press, 2003.

Stafford, William. *The Answers Are Inside the Mountains: Meditations on the Writing Life*. University of Michigan Press, 2003.

Stafford, William. *You Must Revise Your Life*. University of Michigan Press, 1986.

Wilkinson, Joshua Marie, editor. *Poets on Teaching: A Sourcebook*. University of Iowa Press, 2010.

Author

Kyle Vaughn's poems have appeared in numerous literary journals and anthologies, including *Adbusters*, *Vinyl*, *Poetry East*, and Jack Myers's *The Portable Poetry Workshop*. His prose has appeared in *English Journal*, where he won the Paul and Kate Farmer Award for his article "Reading the Literature of War: A Global Perspective on Ethics." His photography has appeared in journals such as *Annalemma*, and *Holon*. In 2012 he collaborated on the book *A New Light in Kalighat*, featuring portraits of and stories about the children of the Kalighat district of Kolkata. He has been an educator since 1998. During his tenure at the Hockaday

Photo by Eli Vaughn

School, Parish Episcopal School, and now Pulaski Academy, where he is currently Department of English Chair, Vaughn has designed and taught a number of courses, including Creative Writing, World Literature, the Literature of War, Music as Literature, Film as Literature, and Visual Literacy. Email him at kylev75@gmail.com or visit his website, www.kylevaughn.org, for publications, workshops, consultation, and other information.

This book was typeset in TheMix and Palatino by Barbara Frazier.

Typefaces used on the cover include Waters Titling and Filosofia.

The book was printed on 50-lb. White Offset paper by Versa Press, Inc.